THE
TOASTER OVEN
COOKBOOK

REVISED EDITION

David Diresta and Joanne Foran

BRISTOL PUBLISHING ENTERPRISES
Hayward, California

A **nitty gritty**® cookbook

Printed in the United States of America.

ISBN 1-55867-326-1

Cover design: Frank J. Paredes

Cover photography: John A. Benson

Food stylist: Randy Mon

Illustrations: James Balkovek

CONTENTS

HOW TO GET THE MOST FROM YOUR TOASTER OVEN

When many people think of toaster ovens, they think of college students, or small apartments, or starter-kitchens. But think again! This versatile appliance is one of the most popular small kitchen appliances on the market today, and every generation of toaster ovens is being produced with new, innovative features that help to make it a permanent fixture in countless kitchens.

The toaster oven deserves its own cookbook. We don't know of another comprehensive cookbook devoted solely to the toaster oven. Each recipe in this collection has been specifically developed to produce exceptional results and remove the tedium of performing routine cooking tasks with dishes that are easy, fun to prepare and delicious to eat.

We first discovered the potential of the toaster oven when, on a vacation, we cautiously attempted to create a memorable full-course dinner with a basic 4-slice toaster oven. The results were beyond our expectations. After a quick visit to the market, in a short time we dined on a plate of mouth-watering bacon-wrapped scallops followed by baked sole with roasted almonds. We finished with a piping-hot fresh fruit crisp made with peaches and strawberries in a cinnamon-oatmeal crust for dessert.

We were inspired to keep cooking. This cookbook is the result — a compilation of tempting recipes, all tested and developed for use in the toaster oven. Most of the recipes are for two servings. The recipes can accommodate a 2-, 4- or 6-slice oven. The standard toaster oven pan measures about 10½ inches by 7 inches, but all of the pans from the various ovens we tested worked well with these recipes. Most recipes will fit in the toaster oven tray or broiler, or individual round or oval casseroles.

THE ADVANTAGES OF TOASTER OVENS

If you're one of the 40 million people who own a toaster oven, you're already aware of how exceptionally well it toasts breads, bagels, muffins and croissants. Unlike the traditional standup toaster, which limits the thickness of baked goods, the toaster oven allows you to place just about any size item on the rack, and it toasts both sides simultaneously. You'll find, after you have reviewed this book, that toasting is not the only job that this versatile appliance does well. It bakes like an oven and broils like a broiler, with surprising professional results that often surpass a standard-sized oven.

Always handy for that college student who's missing a fully equipped kitchen, and perfect for the small apartment with the closet kitchen, it can also be an additional full-service oven that's helpful for preparing meals during the holidays or when you have several dishes to cook and one oven just doesn't seem to be adequate.

Among the many advantages in cooking with a toaster oven:

- It heats up quickly.

- It's more economical than a large oven because it uses less electricity.
- In hot weather, it doesn't heat up the entire kitchen, like a larger oven does.
- Toaster ovens are relatively inexpensive.
- A toaster oven is portable, and can vacation with you in a beach cottage or a ski cabin.
- The clear window allows you to easily watch foods being cooked.
- The "top brown" feature gives you professional results when preparing baked seafoods, chicken, meats, desserts and open-faced sandwiches.
- It's perfect for reheating cooked foods.
- The intense heat produces crusty breads and crisp pizza crusts perfectly.

OVEN FEATURES AND GENERAL DIRECTIONS

The control panel of your toaster oven has an on/off bake control, which includes temperature settings. It has an on/off toaster control. It has a toast color selector and a top brown setting for broiling. It may have an oven light, a signal light, a signal bell, a defrost setting, and a continuous-clean feature. It may have an easy-clean lining.

Your toaster oven comes with an oven pan, a drip tray and a removable toaster rack.

The oven pan can be used as a baking or casserole dish and as a cookie sheet. The drip tray is inserted on the oven pan for broiling, roasting and baking. As illustrated, the drip tray can be placed in an upper or lower position. This will vary depending on the recipe. The metal rack is where you set the breads, bagels and other baked goods for toasting.

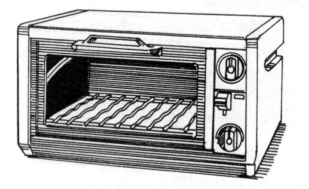

TOASTING

For breads and bagels, set the toaster control to the ON position, set the color selector to the desired degree of darkness and the oven will toast and shut off automatically. On most toaster ovens, a signal bell will ring at the end of the cycle. Some ovens allow you to stop toasting in the middle of a cycle by gently raising the toaster oven control lever or turning the selector dial to OFF.

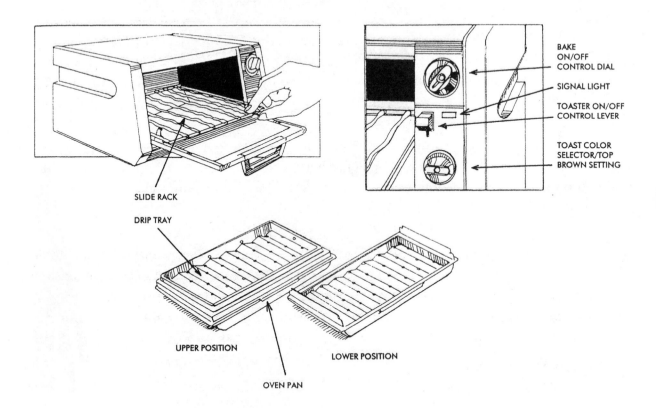

SLIDE RACK

DRIP TRAY

BAKE ON/OFF CONTROL DIAL

SIGNAL LIGHT

TOASTER ON/OFF CONTROL LEVER

TOAST COLOR SELECTOR/TOP BROWN SETTING

UPPER POSITION

LOWER POSITION

OVEN PAN

BROILING

When the recipe calls for broiling, preheat the toaster oven for 1 or 2 minutes with the control set on BROIL. Always watch the food and oven carefully when broiling. Use an insulated pot holder or oven mitt when removing hot pans from the toaster oven. Be sure to keep foods at least 1 inch from the heating element.

BAKING

When baking, set the control dial to the desired temperature. Preheat the oven for 5 minutes, or if your oven is equipped with a signal light, wait for the light to indicate the oven is ready. Turn the control selector to OFF when you finish baking. Be sure to keep foods at least 1 inch from the heating element.

USEFUL EQUIPMENT

Check your local kitchen specialty shops, restaurant supply houses and discount stores, for handy cookware you can use in your toaster oven. Go armed with the inside dimensions of your oven. Many items are coated with easy-care nonstick surfaces. You may find:

- sear and grill pans
- mini muffin and loaf pans
- individual-sized pizza pans
- small baking pans in various sizes
- 10-inch pizza pans—and screens, for crisper crusts
- insulated cookie sheets
- ceramic bakeware

We have also found small individual ramekins, or individual casseroles, to be very useful for toaster oven cooking.

If you plan to make many pizzas in your oven, or crusty breads, you can line the rack with terra cotta tiles to produce the same effect you would get with a pizza (baking) stone. At least one manufacturer includes a pizza stone with the oven.

Finally, we think a good instant-read thermometer is an important device for testing poultry, meats and fish for the best results. The best recipe is no longer good if it is overcooked.

CARING FOR YOUR TOASTER OVEN

Your toaster oven is packaged with a "use and care" book. We strongly recommend that you read it carefully before you start cooking in your oven. Pay special attention to the manufacturer's instructions for the proper way to set it up and the correct method for cooking. Any misuse could possibly void the warranty.

Follow the manufacturer's instructions and clean your toaster oven as often as recommended. Be sure it's shut off, unplugged and cooled down. And don't forget to clean out the crumb tray.

Happy cooking!

APPETIZERS AND SNACKS

SHRIMP AND BROCCOLI PIZZA

The condensed cooking area and intense heat in the toaster oven creates the ideal conditions for baking homemade pizza. It's easy to double this recipe.

PIZZA CRUST
3 cups all purpose flour
$1/2$ tsp. salt
1 pkg. active dry yeast
$1^{1}/_{4}$ cups warm water
olive oil

SHRIMP AND BROCCOLI TOPPING
2 tbs. pizza sauce
2 tbs. Parmesan cheese
2 tbs. Romano cheese
$1/2$ cup fresh or frozen broccoli florets
4 large shrimp, shelled, deveined, uncooked
$1/4$ tsp. oregano dried or 1 tsp. fresh

For the crust, in a large bowl, combine flour, salt, yeast and warm water. Stir together to form a ball. Place on a floured surface and knead for 10 minutes. Place dough in a lightly oiled bowl. Cover with a towel and allow to rise for 1 to $1^{1}/_{2}$ hours, in a warm, draft-free area. Punch down the dough. Form into a ball; cover with a towel and let rest for 30 minutes.

Divide dough into 4 equal portions. Roll out one portion to fit an 8-inch round pizza pan, or place on a baking tray. Refrigerate or freeze remaining pizza dough. Spread tomato sauce over dough and top with cheeses, broccoli, shrimp and oregano. Bake in a preheated 450° oven for 12 to 15 minutes. Makes one individual 8-inch-round pizza.

SHRIMP TOAST TRIANGLES

Servings: 4

This appetizer looks, tastes and smells irresistible. It's perfect to serve at a party. You can prepare the mixture in advance and it takes just a flash to spread it on the toast and heat it in the toaster oven.

6 oz. cooked shrimp, crabmeat or lobster meat
1 clove garlic, minced or pressed
1 tsp. fresh lemon juice
3 tbs. plain nonfat yogurt
$\frac{1}{8}$ tsp. salt
$\frac{1}{8}$ tsp. pepper
4 slices white bread, crusts removed
$\frac{1}{2}$ cup shredded Monterey Jack cheese
1 tsp. chopped fresh basil

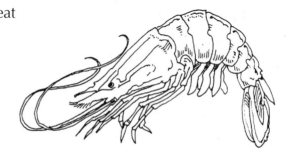

Put cooked shrimp into bite-sized pieces. In a large bowl, mix together shrimp, garlic, lemon juice, yogurt, salt and pepper. Lightly toast bread. Spread shrimp mixture on one side of each slice of toast. Top with shredded cheese. Place on the toaster oven pan and broil until cheese melts. Remove from oven and sprinkle with fresh basil. Cut each slice diagonally into 2 pieces. Serve immediately.

SPICY PITA CHIPS

This treat can be eaten as is and goes well with a glass of wine and a selection of inter-esting fresh fruits, including red and green grapes, strawberries, kiwis, mangoes and papayas. Or serve with a veggie dip or a low fat tomato salsa.

3 pita breads
1/4 cup plain nonfat yogurt
2 cloves garlic, pressed
1/8 tsp. dried oregano
1 tsp. grated Parmesan cheese
1/8 tsp. pepper
1 tsp. olive oil

Split each pita bread at the edges into 2 circles. Cut each circle into 6 wedges. In a small bowl, combine all ingredients, except pita wedges and olive oil. Mix thoroughly. Brush rough side of each pita wedge with a thin coating of yogurt mixture. Lightly coat a cookie sheet or toaster oven tray with olive oil. Place wedges on cookie sheet or oven tray, yogurt side up. Bake in a preheated 300° toaster oven for 30 to 35 minutes, or until lightly brown. Serve hot or cold in a serving basket or bowl.

PESTO PIZZA WITH FRESH TOMATOES

Serves: 8-12

The extra pesto and pizza dough are suitable for freezing. Just freeze the pesto without the Parmesan cheese and add the cheese after the pesto defrosts. The pizza dough can stay in the freezer for up to 4 months and will defrost in a couple of hours at room temperature. If you want round pizza instead of the rectangular ones this recipe describes, you can buy small, individual pizza pans that will fit in your toaster oven. Look in restaurant supply stores and in some discount stores.

PIZZA DOUGH

1 pkg. active dry yeast
1 cup plus 1 tbs. warm water
1 tbs. sugar
2¼ cups all-purpose flour

1 cup whole wheat flour
½ tsp. salt
3 tbs. olive oil

In a small bowl, dissolve yeast in water and add sugar. Set aside for 5 minutes. In a large bowl, combine flours, salt, yeast mixture and 3 tbs. olive oil. Stir together to form a ball. Place dough on a floured surface and knead for 10 minutes. Place dough in a greased bowl. Cover with a towel or plastic wrap and allow to rise for 1 to 1½ hours in a draft-free area. Punch down dough. Form into a ball, cover with a towel or plastic wrap and let rest for 30 minutes.

PESTO

2 cups fresh basil leaves
3 cloves garlic, peeled
1 cup olive oil
½ cup pine nuts or chopped walnuts
¼ tsp. freshly ground pepper
½ cup grated Parmesan cheese

Combine basil, garlic, olive oil, nuts and pepper in a food processor or blender. Process for 15 to 20 seconds or until a paste forms. Pour into a bowl and mix in Parmesan cheese.

4 plum tomatoes, chopped
4 tbs. minced scallions

To assemble pizzas: Divide dough into 4 equal portions. Roll out each portion of dough to fit a lightly oiled 10-x-6-inch oven pan or cookie tray. Spread 3 to 4 tbs. pesto evenly over dough, leaving a ½-inch border around outside edge. Distribute chopped tomato and scallions on pesto. Bake in a preheated 400° toaster oven for 22 minutes. Repeat for remaining dough. Cut into small pieces to serve as appetizers, or into larger pieces for a meal.

SPICY PEPPER CRACKERS

Making your own crackers is fun and easy. This cracker recipe has an assertive flavor. Serve them plain or with assorted spreads, cheeses, dips or soups. Or break up the crackers and add them to salads for croutons.

1/3 cup all-purpose flour
1/2 cup whole wheat flour
1/8 tsp. salt
1/4 tsp. baking powder
3/4 tsp. pepper
3 tbs. butter, room temperature
3 tbs. plain nonfat yogurt
1 tbs. honey

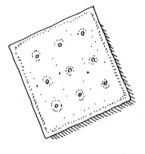

In a large bowl, combine flours, salt, baking powder and pepper. With a pastry cutter, blend in butter, yogurt and honey. Mix well. On a lightly floured surface, roll out dough to 1/8-inch thick. Cut rolled dough into 2-inch squares. Place squares on an ungreased toaster oven pan or small cookie sheet. Bake in a preheated 375° toaster oven for 6 minutes. Turn crackers over and bake for an additional 6 minutes. Serve hot or cold. Store in an airtight container after crackers cool.

STUFFED POTATO SKINS

Reserve the extra potato pulp for Crustless Chicken Pie, *page 72, or mashed potatoes. Just store the pulp in the refrigerator and it will keep for 2 days.*

3 baking potatoes
1 tsp. olive oil
4 strips bacon, cooked and crumbled
1 cup chopped broccoli, steamed for 2 minutes

1/3 cup shredded Monterey Jack, fontina or mozzarella cheese
1/3 cup sour cream, optional
1 tbs. fresh chives, optional

Wash potatoes under cold running water with a stiff vegetable brush. Cut potatoes in half lengthwise. Place potato halves, skin side down, on a lightly greased oven pan. Bake in a preheated 475° toaster oven for 40 minutes. Carefully scoop out pulp, leaving 1/4-inch shells. Brush inside shells with olive oil and cover with equal amounts of bacon, broccoli and cheese. Bake in a preheated 350° toaster oven for 15 minutes. Serve with sour cream and fresh chives.

VARIATION

Stuff skins with cooked chicken, sweet corn niblets, sun-dried tomato pieces and a little sprinkle of dried basil, or a big sprinkle of chopped fresh basil.

CHUNKY TOMATO AND GARLIC BRUSCHETTA

Servings: 2

Serve hot or cold. This is a tasty appetizer for two, or lunch for one. You can prepare it in the toaster oven while dinner is baking in the conventional oven.

3 plum tomatoes
1 clove garlic
2 tbs. high-quality olive oil
$\frac{1}{2}$ tsp. balsamic vinegar
2–3 leaves fresh basil, chopped
1 small French bread loaf
1 tsp. grated Parmesan cheese, optional

Chop tomatoes into $\frac{1}{2}$-inch chunks. Slice garlic into $\frac{1}{8}$-inch slices. In a small bowl, combine tomato, garlic, olive oil, balsamic vinegar and basil. Refrigerate for 2 to 3 hours. Cut French bread in half lengthwise. Place in a toaster oven and toast until lightly brown. Top bread with tomatoes, garlic and basil. Drizzle with any remaining marinade. Sprinkle with Parmesan cheese, if used, and bake in a preheated 350° toaster oven for 10 minutes.

SPICY SPARERIBS

This recipe always gets raves. These can be somewhat messy to eat, but the flavor is well worth it. They're perfect for a casual setting. Just pass lots of napkins!

1½–2 lb. spareribs
½ cup brown sugar, firmly packed
¼ cup light soy sauce
1 tbs. honey
1 tsp. ground ginger
2 cloves garlic, minced or pressed
⅛ tsp. dry mustard

Cut spareribs into individual serving pieces. In a medium bowl, combine all ingredients except spareribs. Place ribs in a shallow bowl. Add marinade and coat all ribs thoroughly. Cover with plastic wrap or foil and refrigerate for 4 hours or overnight. Place ribs on the toaster oven pan. Pour marinade over ribs and cover with foil. Bake in a preheated 350° toaster oven for 1 hour, basting ribs occasionally. Remove foil and bake for an additional 30 minutes. Spoon sauce over ribs and serve.

HERB-FLAVORED BAGEL CHIPS

Makes: 24

This garlicky snack is a great way to use up day-old bagels.

4 plain bagels
2 tbs. butter
¼ cup olive oil
1 clove garlic, minced or pressed
¼ tsp. dried basil

Slice each bagel into 6 slices about ¼-inch thick. Melt butter in a small saucepan. Add oil, garlic and basil and sauté over low heat for 10 minutes. Brush one side of bagel slices with butter-oil mixture. Place bagel slices on an ungreased oven pan, oiled side up. Bake in a preheated 350° toaster oven for 15 to 18 minutes, or until golden brown. Serve hot or cold. Chips will keep fresh for 2 or 3 days in an airtight container.

VARIATIONS

For a breakfast treat, substitute canola oil for olive oil and add 1 tsp. cinnamon and 2 tsp. sugar to melted butter and oil. Brush over bagel slices and bake as directed.

For a bold and hearty flavor, add 1 tbs. dry mustard to butter-oil mixture. Brush over whole wheat bagel slices, sprinkle with 4 tsp. sesame seeds and bake as directed.

BAKED HAM ROLLS

Serve two rolls to each person as an appetizer or slice the rolls into 2-inch pieces, secured with picks, for a buffet.

8 asparagus spears
8 slices baked or boiled ham,
   about ⅛-inch thick

¼ cup shredded Monterey Jack cheese
¼ cup shredded fontina cheese
½ tsp. dried parsley

Cook asparagus in a pot of boiling water for about 6 to 8 minutes, or until tender. Drain well. Lay out ham slices. Place an asparagus spear in the center of each slice. Cover asparagus with equal portions of Monterey Jack and fontina cheeses. Sprinkle with parsley. Roll slices of ham around cheese and asparagus. Place rolls on the toaster oven pan and bake in a preheated 375° toaster oven for 6 to 7 minutes, or until cheese melts. Serve warm.

VARIATION

Roll a slice of prosciutto around a 2-inch piece of cooked asparagus. Omit shredded cheese and drizzle asparagus with *Honey-Mustard Balsamic Vinaigrette,* page 65. Bake as directed.

BACON-WRAPPED SCALLOPS

You'll need 16 three-inch wooden picks for this. To prevent the wooden picks from burning, soak them in water for 20 minutes. The toaster oven allows you to prepare this popular appetizer without disturbing the main course you're cooking in your large oven. Chives are easy to grow — the perennial plant requires little care, and the purple blossoms add a nice extra garnish.

8 scallops, about ¼ lb.   1 tsp. minced fresh chives
4 slices bacon

Rinse scallops under cold water and pat dry. Cut scallops in half. Cut bacon into 2½-inch strips. Wrap a piece of bacon around each scallop. Secure bacon with a wooden pick. Arrange bacon-wrapped scallops on the toaster oven pan and bake in a preheated 400° toaster oven for 20 minutes. Transfer to a serving platter. Sprinkle with fresh chives. Serve warm.

VARIATIONS

Substitute marinated water chestnuts, quartered artichoke hearts or mushrooms for scallops. Marinate water chestnuts and artichoke hearts for 1 hour and mushrooms for 8 hours in 2 tbs. soy sauce, 1 tbs. dry sherry, ¼ tsp. dry mustard and 1 tbs. honey. Bake until bacon is completely cooked and lightly crisp.

BAKED HERB CROUTONS

Tasty croutons are a great way to boost the flavor and add style and texture to a basic green salad or a Caesar salad. They're also good for just munching!

3 slices 1-inch-thick, day-old bread, French or Italian
2 tbs. butter
1/4 tsp. dried lemon peel

1/4 tsp. dried dill weed
1/8 tsp. dried parsley
1 clove garlic, minced or pressed, optional
freshly ground pepper to taste

Cut bread slices into 1/2-inch or 3/4-inch cubes and do not remove crusts. Melt butter in a nonstick skillet over medium heat and add herbs. Place cubes of bread in the skillet and reduce heat to medium low. Sauté for 4 to 5 minutes, stirring constantly. Place croutons on the toaster oven pan and bake in a preheated 325° toaster oven for 25 minutes. Turn occasionally until lightly golden brown.

VARIATION

Make pizza-flavored croutons by substituting dried basil and oregano for lemon peel and dill.

ROASTED GARLIC ROLL-UPS

This is one recipe that everybody will want. The flavor of roasted garlic is surprisingly mild and nutty. Try it on crusty breads in place of butter — it's healthier and tastes better.

ROASTED GARLIC
1 bulb garlic
1/4 tsp.-1 tbs. olive oil
1 tsp. butter, optional
1/8 tsp. dried oregano
1/8 tsp. dried thyme
1/4 tsp. pepper
1/4 tsp. dried basil
1 tbs. plus 1 tsp. olive oil
1 tbs. diced jalapeño pepper
1 tbs. grated Parmesan cheese
4 flour tortillas, 8-inch diameter
8 thin slices salami
1 jar (7.5 oz.) roasted red bell peppers, cut into 1-inch strips

To roast garlic, cut ¼ inch from top of garlic bulb. Remove loose outer leaves. Bulb should remain intact. Place garlic on a small sheet of foil. Pour ¼ tsp. olive oil over bulb and dot with butter, or pour 1 tbs. olive oil over bulb and eliminate butter. Sprinkle with oregano, thyme and pepper. Seal foil and bake in a preheated 350° toaster oven for 50 minutes.

Separate cloves and squeeze out garlic. Mash garlic and combine with basil, 1 tbs. olive oil, jalapeño pepper and cheese in a medium bowl and mix well. Lay out tortillas. Spread filling on tortillas, leaving a ½-inch border. Place 2 slices salami on each tortilla. Evenly distribute a layer of roasted peppers on top of salami. Roll up tortillas to create logs. Brush tops with 1 tsp. olive oil. Place on the toaster oven pan and bake in a preheated 400° toaster oven for 15 minutes. Remove from oven, let cool for 5 to 10 minutes and slice into 1-inch pieces. Serve warm on wooden picks.

INDIVIDUAL MEXICAN PIZZAS

Servings: 2

These pizzas cook very quickly. If you're serving two, just cut the first cooked pizza in half and you'll be ready to eat the second one as soon as it's done.

2 flour or whole wheat tortillas, 8-inch diameter
1/2 tsp. vegetable oil
1/2 cup mashed refried beans
1/4 cup chopped tomatoes
1/8 cup sliced black olives
1/4 cup chopped onion
1/4 cup chopped red bell pepper
1 tbs. thinly sliced jalapeño pepper
1/2 cup shredded Monterey Jack cheese or reduced fat cheddar cheese
salsa or sour cream, optional

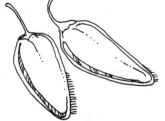

Heat tortillas, one at a time, in a preheated 400° toaster oven for 1 1/2 minutes. Brush each tortilla with oil. Cover each tortilla with a layer of beans and top with tomatoes, olives, onion, red bell pepper and jalapeño slices. Sprinkle with cheese. Bake in 400° toaster oven for 13 minutes, or until cheese is melted. Serve immediately with salsa or sour cream.

ANCHOVY AND CHEESE CANAPÉS

If you're serving a large group of people, increase the recipe — but you may want to make only half with anchovies.

6 slices white bread
2 tbs. butter, softened
1 clove garlic, minced or pressed
1/4 tsp. dried basil
1/8 tsp. pepper
6 thin slices mozzarella cheese, cut into 3-inch rounds
1 large tomato, cut into 6 slices
1 anchovy fillet, cut into small pieces
1/4 tsp. dried oregano

Lightly toast bread. Cut a round disk out of each slice using a 3-inch cookie cutter or the rim of a glass. In a small bowl, blend together butter, garlic, basil and pepper. Spread equal portions of mixture on toast round. Cover with a slice of cheese and top with a slice of tomato and a piece of anchovy. Sprinkle with oregano. Bake in a preheated 350° toaster oven for 12 to 15 minutes, or until cheese melts. Serve immediately.

CHEESY BACON SPINACH PUFFS

When it comes to looks and taste, these little gems are a sure hit every time.

1 frozen unbaked puff pastry sheet
1 tbs. vegetable oil
1/2 cup chopped cooked spinach, well drained
1/4 cup shredded mozzarella cheese
3 strips bacon, cooked and crumbled
2 tbs. cold water

Thaw sheet of pastry for 30 minutes. Use a rolling pin to roll pastry into a 12-inch square. Divide pastry into sixteen 3-inch squares. Brush each square with oil. In a medium bowl, combine spinach, cheese and bacon. Mix thoroughly. Divide mixture evenly among squares, about 1 tbs. on one corner of each oiled pastry square. Fold over the opposite corner to create a triangle. Seal and crimp edges with a fork. Place spinach puffs on a lightly oiled toaster oven pan. Brush tops with cold water and bake in a preheated 400° toaster oven for 15 minutes. Remove from oven, let cool and serve.

KEY LIME NACHOS

When she's not actively working on cookbooks, Joanne can be found preparing mouth-watering dishes like this popular appetizer at The Top Of The Scales restaurant in historic North Andover, Massachusetts. The recipe works exceptionally well in a toaster oven. For variety, substitute fresh lemon juice for the lime juice. The recipe is written for a standard 4-slice toaster oven, but can easily be adapted for larger quantities. Use a reduced fat cheddar if you prefer.

2 oz. tortilla chips
1½ tsp. fresh Key lime juice or regular lime juice
½ cup shredded Monterey Jack cheese
½ tsp. chili powder
1 dash cayenne pepper

Spread ½ of the tortilla chips evenly on the toaster oven pan. Drizzle chips with ½ of the lime juice and cover chips with ½ of the cheese. Spread remaining chips over cheese. Drizzle remaining lime juice and cover with remaining cheese. Sprinkle with chili powder and cayenne pepper. Bake in a preheated 400° toaster oven for 5 to 6 minutes. Serve immediately.

STUFFED PORTOBELLO MUSHROOMS

Serve as an appetizer or as a side dish with chicken or seafood.

2 portobello mushrooms, each cut into
    4 vertical slices about 1/2-inch thick
1 tbs. butter
1 clove garlic, minced or pressed
1 small onion, finely chopped
1/4 tsp. dried thyme

1/4 tsp. dried sage
6 oz. sausage meat
1 tbs. seasoned breadcrumbs
1 tsp. grated Romano cheese
1 tsp. olive oil
1/4 tsp. dried basil

Use a sharp paring knife to carve out an indentation for the filling in each mushroom slice, being careful not to cut through the sides and bottoms. Set prepared mushrooms aside and chop centers into small pieces. Melt butter in a medium skillet. Add garlic, onion, thyme and sage. Cook over medium heat until onion is soft. Add chopped mushrooms. Add sausage and sauté for 5 minutes, or until meat is cooked and crumbled. Stir in breadcrumbs and Romano cheese. Lightly coat the toaster oven pan with nonstick vegetable spray. While sausage is cooking, place mushrooms on toaster oven pan. Brush top side with oil and broil for 1 minute. Spread 1/4-inch layer of cooked sausage mixture on mushroom slices. Sprinkle with basil. Bake in a preheated 350° toaster oven for 7 minutes. Carefully remove from oven; serve warm.

POPCORN SWEETS

You'll recognize this crunchy, sweet, old-fashioned snack. It stores well in an airtight container.

2½ cups popped corn, unbuttered and unsalted
2 tsp. light maple syrup
1 tbs. plus 1 tsp. butter
3 tbs. brown sugar
½ tsp. white sugar
3 tbs. peanuts
⅛ tsp. vanilla extract
⅛ tsp. baking soda

Lightly coat a 9-x-6-x-1-inch pan with cooking spray or vegetable oil. Spread popcorn evenly in pan and set aside. Combine maple syrup, butter, brown sugar, granulated sugar and peanuts in a small saucepan. Bring to a boil and reduce heat to medium, stirring continuously for 2 minutes. Add vanilla and baking soda. Remove from heat, mix quickly and pour over popcorn. Stir carefully to coat all popcorn. Bake in a preheated 275° toaster oven for 20 minutes. Remove from oven. Pour into a serving bowl, let cool and serve.

FRUIT-FILLED TREATS

Makes: 6

This recipe is simple to prepare, and makes a kind of instant tart, hot and tasty.

3 flour tortillas, 8-inch diameter
3 tsp. favorite fruit preserves

$^1/_2$ tsp. cold water
$^1/_2$ tsp. sugar

Cut each tortilla in half. Spread $^1/_2$ tsp. fruit preserves on each half, leaving a 1-inch border. Fold in half to create a triangle. Press a fork against edges to crimp and seal. Place tarts on a toaster oven pan. Drizzle with water and sprinkle with sugar. Prick tops with a fork. Bake in a preheated 350° toaster oven for 8 to 10 minutes. Serve warm.

CINNAMON TORTILLA CHIPS

Makes: 12

These nibbles go nicely with sandwich and salad—or as dessert, with coffee or cappuccino.

2 small flour tortillas
$^1/_2$ tsp. sugar

$^1/_8$ tsp. cinnamon or cocoa

Cut each tortilla into 6 wedges. Place wedges on the toaster oven tray. Sprinkle with sugar and cinnamon or cocoa. Bake in a preheated 350° toaster oven for 7 minutes, or until crisp.

PICANTE SALSA

Serve with nachos and tacos or spread over cooked chicken, fish or frankfurters.

3/4 cup chopped ripe tomatoes
1 clove garlic, minced or pressed
1 small onion, finely chopped
2 tbs. chopped jalapeño pepper
1/2 tbs. chili powder
1 tsp. fresh lemon juice
1/2 tsp. red wine vinegar
1/4 cup finely chopped green bell
   pepper

In a large bowl, combine all ingredients. Mix thoroughly and refrigerate for at least 2 hours.

QUICK BREADS AND YEAST BREADS

ORANGE POPPY SEED MINI LOAVES

You'll be amazed and delighted at the quality of flavor, texture and appearance of these mini loaves.

1 cup all-purpose flour
1 tsp. baking powder
$^2/_3$ cup sugar
1 egg white
3 tbs. butter, melted

6 tbs. milk
2 tbs. orange juice
$^3/_4$ tsp. grated fresh orange peel (zest)
$^1/_8$ tsp. cinnamon
$^3/_4$ tsp. poppy seeds

In a large bowl, combine flour, baking powder and sugar. Add egg white, butter and milk and use an electric mixer to blend. Add orange juice, orange zest, cinnamon and poppy seeds. Mix well. Spray 2 mini loaf pans (3$^1/_2$-x-6-x-2 inches) lightly with nonstick vegetable spray. Pour batter into pans. Bake in a preheated 350° toaster oven for 25 minutes. Let cool and cut into $^1/_2$-inch slices.

VARIATION: LEMON POPPY SEED MINI LOAVES

Substitute lemon zest and lemon juice for the orange zest and orange juice.

OATMEAL RAISIN SQUARES

One batch of these great-tasting thick squares prepared in the toaster oven is enough for a crowd.

1/4 cup butter, softened
1/4 cup granulated sugar
1/4 cup brown sugar, firmly packed
1 egg
1/2 tsp. vanilla extract
1 cup flour

1/2 tsp. cinnamon
1/4 tsp. baking soda
1 cup oats
1/4 cup raisins
1/4 cup molasses
1/4 cup chopped walnuts

With an electric mixer, cream together butter and sugars. Add egg and vanilla. Mix well. In a medium bowl, combine flour, cinnamon, baking soda and oats. Mix well and add to butter and sugar mixture. Add raisins, molasses and walnuts. Mix well. Lightly coat the toaster oven pan with vegetable cooking spray. Firmly press dough evenly into toaster oven pan. Bake in a preheated 350° toaster oven for 15 to 17 minutes, or until a wooden pick inserted in the center comes out clean. Let cool for 10 minutes. Cut into 24 squares.

VANILLA ALMOND COFFEE CAKE

Makes: 2 loaves

This luscious snack really qualifies as a dessert: perfect after dinner with coffee or tea.

³/₄ cup butter, softened
1 cup sugar
1 egg
¹/₂ tbs. vanilla extract

1 cup plain low fat yogurt
1 tsp. baking powder
1¹/₃ cups flour

Cream together ³/₄ cup softened butter and sugar. Add egg, vanilla and yogurt. Add baking powder and flour. Mix well. Lightly grease two 3¹/₂-x-6-x-2-inch mini loaf pans. Pour equal amounts of batter into pans.

TOPPING

2 tbs. butter
¹/₄ cup sugar
1 tsp. cinnamon

¹/₈ cup flour
¹/₄ tsp. ground cardamom
2 tbs. sliced almonds

Combine all ingredients except almonds in a bowl. Use your hands to mix thoroughly until mixture looks like peas. Divide in half and sprinkle over cake batter. Sprinkle with sliced almonds. Bake in a preheated 350° toaster oven for 45 minutes. Let cool and cut into slices.

MINI CARROT CAKE MUFFINS

To assure the best tasting muffins, use only fresh, natural ingredients and stay away from artificial vanilla. Try serving these with cappuccino or cafe latte.

$2/3$ cup grated carrots
2 tbs. warm water
$1/3$ cup all-purpose flour
$1/3$ cup whole wheat flour
$1/2$ tsp. baking soda
4 tsp. sugar
8 tsp. vegetable oil

1 egg white
$1/2$ tsp. vanilla extract
$1/2$ tsp. cinnamon
$1/8$ tsp. ground cloves
8 tsp. maple syrup
1 tbs. raisins
2 tbs. finely chopped walnuts

In a large bowl, combine carrots and water. Sift in flours and baking soda. Mix well. Add sugar, oil, egg white, vanilla, spices and maple syrup. Mix well but do not overmix. Fold in raisins. Lightly coat a 12-cup mini muffin pan or a regular 6-cup muffin pan with nonstick vegetable spray. Pour batter into muffin cups and sprinkle tops with nuts. Bake in a preheated 350° toaster oven for 20 to 22 minutes, or until golden brown. Cool on a wire rack.

ZUCCHINI MUFFINS

A 12-cup mini muffin pan will fit in all 4-slice toaster ovens, and can be found at most kitchenware shops.

³/₄ cup shredded zucchini
2 tbs. honey
2 tbs. plus 2 tsp. vegetable oil
1 egg white
¼ tsp. vanilla extract
³/₄ cup flour

¼ tsp. baking soda
¼ tsp. baking powder
½ tsp. cinnamon
⅛ tsp. ground cloves
¼ cup finely chopped walnuts

In a large bowl, combine zucchini, honey, oil, egg white and vanilla; mix well. In a medium bowl, combine flour, baking soda, baking powder, cinnamon, cloves and nuts. Mix well. Add dry ingredients to zucchini mixture and mix until just moistened. Lightly coat a 12-cup mini muffin pan, or a regular 6-cup pan, with nonstick vegetable spray. Pour batter into muffin cups. Bake in a preheated 350° toaster oven for 25 minutes. Remove from pan and let cool.

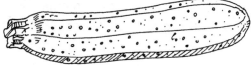

COFFEE CAKE MUFFINS

You can serve these any time of the day, from breakfast to an after-dinner dessert with coffee or tea.

1/4 cup butter, softened	1 cup ricotta cheese
1/2 cup sugar	1 cup all-purpose flour
1 egg	1 1/2 tsp. baking powder
3/4 tsp. vanilla extract	2 tbs. skim milk

In a medium bowl, cream together butter and sugar. Add egg, vanilla and ricotta cheese. Mix well. Slowly add flour, baking powder and milk. Mix well.

TOPPING

1/3 cup finely chopped walnuts	1 tsp. cinnamon
2 tsp. sugar	1/8 tsp. nutmeg

In a small bowl, mix together all topping ingredients. Lightly spray a 6-cup muffin pan with nonstick vegetable spray. Pour 1/2 of the batter into muffin cups. Sprinkle 1/2 of the topping over batter. Pour remaining batter into muffin cups and cover with remaining topping. Bake in a preheated 350° toaster oven for 40 to 45 minutes, or until muffin tops are golden brown.

CURRANT ALMOND MUFFINS

The almonds and currants blend together nicely for a moist and flavorful muffin. They're good warm or at room temperature.

3/4 cup all-purpose flour
3 tbs. finely chopped almonds
1/2 tsp. baking powder
1/8 tsp. salt
1 egg, beaten
2 tbs. honey
2 tbs. vegetable oil
1/2 tsp. lemon juice
1/4 tsp. vanilla extract
1/3 cup dried currants

In a large bowl, combine flour, almonds, baking powder and salt. Add egg, honey, oil, lemon juice and vanilla and stir until dry ingredients are just moistened. Fold in currants. Lightly coat a 12-cup mini muffin pan or 6-cup muffin pan with nonstick vegetable spray. Pour equal amounts of batter into muffin cups. Bake in a preheated 350° toaster oven for 20 to 22 minutes. Let cool.

COLONIAL CINNAMON NUT BREAD

Makes: 4 loaves

The aroma of freshly baked bread creates a feeling of friendship and hospitality. This bread is so richly delicious it can be sliced and served as a dessert. Begin by preparing the filling.

FILLING

1/2 cup finely chopped walnuts
1/4 cup sugar
1 1/2 tsp. cinnamon
1 tbs. ricotta cheese

In a small bowl, combine walnuts, sugar, cinnamon and ricotta cheese. Mix well and set aside.

DOUGH

1 pkg. active dry yeast
1 cup plus 2 tbs. warm water
4 tsp. sugar
3 1/4 cups all-purpose flour
1 tbs. shortening

In a small bowl, dissolve yeast in water and add 4 tsp. sugar. Set aside. In a large bowl, combine 2 cups flour and shortening with an electric mixer. Add yeast mixture and mix well. Stir in enough of the remaining flour to make dough easy to handle. Place dough in a greased bowl and turn to grease completely. Cover with plastic wrap, set in a warm location and let rise for 1 hour or until dough doubles in size.

Punch down dough and divide into 4 equal portions. Roll out each portion in a 6-x-9-inch rectangle. Sprinkle entire surface of rectangle with filling.

To shape bread loaves: For each rectangle, fold like a business letter, covering the center third with the left third, and then the right third. The dough should now measure about 3 x 6 inches. Starting on the wide side, roll up dough to form a long loaf. Pinch edges to seal. Fold ends under loaf, about 1 inch or so. Repeat with remaining dough. Place loaves in 3½-x-6-x-2-inch bread pans and bake in a preheated 400° toaster oven for 35 minutes. Remove bread loaves from pans and cool on a wire rack.

CHEESY SOFT PRETZELS

Makes: 8

Serve hot or cold, with or without mustard. For variety, use 1 cup whole wheat flour and 2 cups all-purpose flour to make whole wheat pretzels.

1 pkg. active dry yeast
1 cup warm water
1 tsp. sugar
3 cups all-purpose flour

1/4 tsp. salt
1 egg white
1tsp. grated Parmesan cheese

In a small bowl, dissolve yeast in water and add sugar. Set aside for 5 minutes. In a large bowl, combine flour, salt and yeast mixture. Stir yeast mixture with dry ingredients to form a ball. Place dough on a floured surface and knead for 10 minutes. Place dough in a greased bowl and turn to grease completely. Cover with a towel or plastic wrap and allow to rise for 1½ hours in a warm, draft-free area. Punch down dough and allow to rest for 10 minutes. Divide dough into 8 equal pieces and roll each piece into an 18-inch-long rope. Cross one end of each rope over the other and twist the ends over again. Fold twisted ends toward bottom of loop to form pretzel.

Coat the toaster oven pan with nonstick vegetable spray. Place 4 pretzels on pan; brush with egg white and sprinkle with cheese. Bake in a preheated 450° toaster oven for 15 to 18 minutes, or until golden brown. Repeat with remaining 4 pretzels.

MINI FRENCH BREAD LOAVES

Makes: 4 loaves

This bread is remarkably good and is ideal for baking in any size toaster oven. The crust is crisp and the center is moist and flavorful. You can store the loaves in the freezer wrapped first in plastic and then in aluminum foil for up to two months.

1 pkg. active dry yeast
2½ cups warm water
1½ tsp. salt

7 cups all-purpose flour
½ tsp. cornmeal

In a large bowl, dissolve yeast in all of the water and set aside for 5 minutes. Add salt and flour, 1 cup at a time, and mix together to form a ball. Place dough on a floured surface and knead for 10 minutes. Place dough in a greased bowl and turn to grease completely. Cover with a towel or plastic wrap and allow to rise in a draft-free area for 1½ hours or until double in size.

Punch down dough and divide into 4 equal portions. Roll each portion into a 2-x-7-inch loaf. Sprinkle the toaster oven pan with cornmeal and place 2 loaves on pan. Cover loaves with a towel or plastic wrap and let rise for 25 minutes. With a sharp knife, make 2 long ⅛-inch-deep slits on top of each loaf. Brush with cold water and bake in a preheated 450° toaster oven for 15 minutes. Reduce heat to 375° and bake for 20 more minutes. Cool on a wire rack. Bake 2 remaining loaves.

VEGETABLES AND SIDE DISHES

SWEET ONION AND SPINACH FRITTATA

The secret to this mouthwatering recipe is the combination of flavors: the sweet onions and spinach with the eggs and freshly grated Parmesan cheese.

1 small Vidalia or other sweet onion, thinly sliced
one 10 oz. pkg. frozen spinach, thawed and drained
6 eggs
1/4 cup milk
1/4 cup Parmesan cheese, freshly grated
salt and pepper to taste

In a small skillet, heat olive oil over medium heat. Add onions and sauté for 3 to 4 minutes, or until translucent. Remove from heat.

In a large bowl, beat eggs with milk until well mixed. Combine onions, spinach, cheese, salt and pepper with eggs and milk. Pour into a lightly greased 9-inch ovenproof glass or porcelain pie plate.

Bake in a preheated 350° oven for 25 to 30 minutes. Cut into wedges and serve warm.

CURRY ROASTED SWEET POTATOES AND ONIONS

Serve these healthy and delicious rich colored potatoes and onions as a side dish to grilled salmon or baked haddock.

2 medium sweet potatoes, peeled, cut into $1\frac{1}{2}$ inch pieces
1 medium Vidalia or other sweet onion, cut into 1-inch pieces
2 tbs. olive oil
$\frac{1}{4}$ tsp. curry powder
$\frac{1}{2}$ tsp. ground cumin

Combine all ingredients in a baking dish or toaster oven pan and toss well to coat.
Bake in a preheated 425° toaster oven for 35 minutes, or until tender. Stir occasionally. Keep warm until ready to serve.

SOUTHWESTERN FLAVORED COUSCOUS

Servings: 4

This appetizing recipe is mildly spicy and filled with delicious flavors and rich colors. Serve chilled for a perfect accompaniment to fish or chicken.

1 cup dry couscous
2¼ cups chicken stock
2 cloves garlic, minced or pressed
1 cup chopped red or green bell peppers
1 cup sliced mushrooms
½ cup fresh or canned corn kernels

½ cup chopped carrots
¼ tsp. ground cumin
1 tsp. chili powder
salt and pepper to taste
2 tbs. olive oil
¼ cup chopped scallions

Spread couscous on a toaster oven baking sheet and roast in a preheated 425° oven for 7 to 9 minutes, or until golden brown. Remove from oven and pour into a large bowl. In a small saucepan, bring chicken stock to a boil. Pour stock over couscous and set aside until all liquid is absorbed, about 10 to 12 minutes. In a large bowl, combine garlic, peppers, mushrooms, corn, carrots, cumin, chili powder, salt, pepper and olive oil and mix well. Spread vegetables on a toaster oven baking dish and roast at 13 to 15 minutes at 425°. Remove from oven, add to couscous and mix well. Stir in scallions.

ROASTED ASPARAGUS AND CARROTS

Servings: 2

Roasting the asparagus and carrots in a toaster oven intensifies the flavors.

10 asparagus spears
2 medium carrots
2 tbs. olive oil
2 tbs. fresh lemon juice
1 tbs. balsamic vinegar
salt and pepper to taste

Snap off the tough ends of asparagus. Cut each carrot into 4 pieces, lengthwise. Place asparagus spears and carrots on a toaster oven pan. Drizzle with olive oil, lemon juice and balsamic vinegar; sprinkle with salt and pepper. Toss to coat well.

Roast in a preheated 400° toaster oven for 15 minutes. Turn occasionally.

ZUCCHINI CASSEROLE

Servings: 2

Here's another recipe to add to your zucchini file. This delicious vegetable casserole is a good choice for a summer evening and it's also a good way to use up all those vegetables. Serve it with pasta or as a side dish.

1 tbs. butter
1 Vidalia onion, thinly sliced and separated
1/4 tsp. dried basil
1/8 tsp. salt
1/8 tsp. pepper

2 small zucchini, cut into 1/4-inch rounds
1 medium tomato, cut into 1-inch chunks
1 cup thinly sliced mushrooms
1/2 cup shredded Havarti cheese
1 tbs. breadcrumbs

Melt butter in a skillet. Add onion, basil, salt and pepper. Sauté for 5 minutes, or until onion is soft. In a large bowl, combine zucchini, tomato, mushrooms and sautéed onion. Mix well. Divide in half and spoon into 2 individual ovenproof baking dishes. Top with cheese and sprinkle with breadcrumbs. Bake in a preheated 375° toaster oven for 30 minutes. Serve warm.

VEGETABLE LASAGNA

Some foods just seem to attract a wide range of interest. Certainly lasagna is one of them. This version has an appealing combination of flavor, color and texture. You will need an 11½-x-9-x-1-inch pan, which will fit into a 6-slice toaster oven.

6 oz. dried lasagna noodles, about 9 strips
1½ cups broccoli florets
1¾ cups tomato sauce
5 oz. fresh or frozen spinach, cooked and
    well drained

¾ cup shredded carrots
4 oz. fontina cheese, shredded
4½ tsp. grated Parmesan cheese
¼ tsp. dried basil

Cook lasagna noodles according to the instructions on the package and drain. Steam broccoli for 2 minutes, or until bright green. Spread a thin coating of tomato sauce on the bottom of the pan. Place a layer of lasagna noodles over sauce. Spread cooked spinach on lasagna noodles. Spread shredded carrots evenly over spinach. Sprinkle 2 oz. cheese over carrots and spinach. Cover with a layer of lasagna noodles and cover noodles with ¾ cup tomato sauce. Spread broccoli over sauce and top with a layer of lasagna noodles. Spread remaining sauce over noodles and cover with remaining cheeses. Sprinkle with basil. Bake in a preheated 350° toaster oven for 35 minutes.

RAINBOW VEGETABLE ROAST

This is a delicious dish to serve over cooked rice or pasta for a attractive, low fat meal. Tender-skinned summer squash include zucchini, yellow crookneck and pattypan, the one that looks like a flattened top with scalloped edges. Pattypan comes in pale green and yellow. You can use any summer squash in this recipe.

1/4 cup balsamic vinegar
1/8 cup olive oil
1/4 tsp. dried oregano
1/4 tsp. dried basil
1/4 tsp. Old Bay seasoning
2 cups peeled, cubed eggplant, 1-inch cubes

1 small zucchini, cut into 1/4-inch rounds
1 small pattypan squash, cut into 1/4-inch rounds
1 cup chopped broccoli
1 small red onion, thinly sliced and separated
cooked rice or pasta, optional

In a small bowl, combine vinegar, olive oil, oregano, basil and Old Bay seasoning. Mix well and set aside. In a large bowl, combine eggplant, squashes, broccoli and red onion. Pour dressing over vegetables and mix well. Lightly coat the oven pan with nonstick vegetable spray. Spread vegetables and all the dressing in the oven pan and bake in a preheated 475° toaster oven for 45 minutes. Stir occasionally. Then broil for 3 minutes. Serve over cooked rice or pasta if desired.

TOASTER OVEN QUICHE

This crustless quiche makes an ideal accompaniment to a cup of hearty, nourishing soup. Mini quiche pans will fit in any size toaster oven. You'll have plenty of quiche for 2 servings.

1 tsp. butter
1 small onion, finely chopped
2 eggs
1/2 cup milk
1/8 tsp. chili powder

1/8 tsp. salt
1/8 tsp. pepper
3 slices bacon, cooked crisp and crumbled
1/4 cup shredded smoked cheddar cheese

Melt butter in a skillet. Add onion and sauté for about 6 minutes, or until onion is soft. Remove from heat and set aside. In a medium bowl, whisk together eggs, milk, chili powder, salt and pepper. Add crumbled bacon, onion and cheese. Mix thoroughly. Lightly coat 4 mini 4-inch quiche pans or tart tins with nonstick vegetable spray. Pour mixture evenly into pans. Bake in a preheated 350° toaster oven for 60 minutes. Remove from pans. Serve at room temperature or refrigerate and serve chilled.

ROASTED RED-SKINNED POTATOES

Servings: 2

Cinnamon adds an interesting flavor element that produces an exceptional potato dish, and with minimal work. You can serve this any time of the year with seafood, meat or poultry.

6 small new red-skinned potatoes
2 tsp. olive oil
1/4 tsp. cinnamon
1/8 tsp. salt
1/8 tsp. pepper
1 tbs. chopped fresh chives

Wash potatoes under cold running water with a stiff vegetable brush. Remove eyes, but do not peel. Cut into 1- or 1½-inch cubes. Place potato cubes in a medium bowl. Add olive oil, cinnamon, salt, pepper and chives. Stir well, coating all sides of potatoes. Spread potatoes on the toaster oven pan in a single layer. Bake in a preheated 400° toaster oven for 45 minutes. Turn occasionally. Lower oven temperature to 175° and keep potatoes warm until ready to serve.

BAKED ZITI WITH SPINACH

This easy-to-prepare pasta dish has just the right combination of ingredients for great flavor and color. As a time-saver, you can prepare it 2 days in advance. Just keep it covered and stored in the refrigerator before cooking. Serve as a main course with a fresh garden salad and garlic bread, or as a side dish.

1¾ cups dried ziti noodles
1½ cups tomato sauce
3 oz. fresh or frozen spinach, cooked and
  well drained
1 can (14.5 oz.) stewed tomatoes, chopped,
  with juice

2 tbs. grated Parmesan cheese, optional
½ tsp. dried basil
¼ tsp. dried oregano
¼ tsp. dried parsley
¼ tsp. dried rosemary
⅛ tsp. pepper

Cook ziti according to the instructions on the package; drain. In a large bowl, combine cooked pasta and remaining ingredients. Mix thoroughly. Divide pasta mixture into 2 small oval or round ovenproof casseroles. Bake in a preheated 350° oven for 25 minutes.

VARIATION

Add 1 can (6 oz.) white tuna packed in water, drained and flaked.

TUNA-STUFFED POTATOES

Serve this delicious combination as a side dish or as a new and different lunch idea.

2 large potatoes, baked
1 can (16⅛ oz.) white tuna
2 tbs. mayonnaise
2 tbs. finely chopped celery
2 tbs. finely chopped onion

2 tsp. sweet relish
⅛ tsp. salt
⅛ tsp. pepper
12 zucchini slices, ¼-inch rounds
4 slices Muenster cheese

Slice potatoes in half lengthwise and scoop out pulp, leaving a ¼-inch shell. Be careful not to tear shells. Reserve potato pulp for other recipes. Set shells aside. In a large bowl, combine tuna, mayonnaise, celery, onion, relish, salt and pepper. Mix well. Fill potato shells with tuna mixture and top with zucchini slices. Cover with cheese and bake in a preheated 350° toaster oven for 15 minutes. Serve immediately.

VARIATION
Substitute tomato slices for the zucchini.

VEGETABLES AND SIDE DISHES   55

SWISS CHARD AND MUSHROOM CASSEROLE

Here's an appealing spicy dish that's ideal to prepare and serve on a chilly winter day. You can substitute spinach, broccoli, rabe or mustard greens for the Swiss chard.

1 tsp. olive oil
1 small onion, finely chopped
1 clove garlic, minced or pressed
1 cup sliced mushrooms
4 cups chopped Swiss chard, firmly packed
$3/4$ cup water
1 chicken bouillon cube
$1\frac{1}{2}$ cups cooked rice ($\frac{1}{2}$ cup raw)

2 egg whites
2 tbs. grated Parmesan cheese
$\frac{1}{4}$ tsp. dried thyme
$\frac{1}{8}$ tsp. pepper
$\frac{1}{8}$ tsp. salt, optional
$\frac{1}{4}$ tsp. ground dill seed
$\frac{1}{4}$ tsp. paprika

Heat oil in a skillet over medium-low heat. Add onion and garlic and sauté for 2 minutes. Add mushrooms and sauté for 5 minutes. Add Swiss chard and sauté for 3 to 4 minutes. Add water and bouillon cube, bring to a boil and remove from heat. In a large bowl, combine all ingredients, except paprika, and mix well. Pour mixture into 2 round or oval ovenproof casseroles. Bake in a preheated 350° toaster oven for 40 minutes. Remove from oven, sprinkle with paprika and serve warm.

MACARONI AND HAVARTI CHEESE

Macaroni and cheese is one of the twelve most popular main dishes in the United States. Here is our version — it looks and tastes delicious.

1 cup dried elbow macaroni
2 tsp. butter
2 tsp. flour
salt and pepper to taste
²/₃ cup milk
³/₄ cup shredded Danish-style Havarti cheese
½ tsp. dried dill weed, or 1½ tsp. fresh
1 tsp. fine breadcrumbs

Cook macaroni according to the instructions on the package. Drain and set aside. Melt butter in a saucepan over medium heat. Add flour, salt and pepper. Stir continuously and cook for 2 minutes. Add milk and continue to stir until sauce thickens. Remove pan from heat. Stir in cheese until melted. Add macaroni and dill and mix well. Pour macaroni mixture into 2 ungreased 5-inch round ovenproof casseroles. Sprinkle with breadcrumbs. Bake in a preheated 350° toaster oven for 25 to 30 minutes, or until golden brown.

ELEPHANT FRIES

This is a superb method for preparing potatoes in the toaster oven. These are particularly good with burgers and baked chicken. Serve plain or with a dipping sauce as a side dish or appetizer.

2 large baking potatoes
1½ tsp. olive oil
¼ tsp. chili powder
dash cayenne pepper

Carefully wash potatoes. Do not remove skins. Cut each potato into 8 wedges. Whisk together oil, chili powder and cayenne pepper. Brush each wedge with oil mixture. Lightly coat the toaster oven drip tray with nonstick vegetable spray. Place drip tray in the lower position on the oven pan. Place wedges on the drip tray and bake in a preheated 450° toaster oven for 35 to 40 minutes, or until golden brown.

VARIATION: GARLICKY ELEPHANT FRIES

Sauté 1 small crushed garlic clove in 1½ tsp. olive oil for 1 minute. Brush potato wedges with flavored oil and baked as directed.

LASAGNA ROLL-UPS

Servings: 2

This makes dinner for two or a super item to add to a friendly buffet. The flavors are delightful and the generous portions are filling.

4 oz. dried lasagna noodles, about 6 strips
1 pkg. (10 oz.) frozen spinach, cooked and
   well drained
1 cup finely chopped broccoli florets
1 cup ricotta cheese

3/4 cup shredded Monterey Jack cheese
1/2 cup plus 2 tbs. grated Parmesan cheese
1 1/4 cups tomato sauce
1/4 tsp. dried basil

Cook lasagna noodles according to the instructions on the package; drain. In a large bowl, combine spinach, broccoli, ricotta cheese, Monterey Jack cheese and 1/2 cup Parmesan cheese. Mix well. Spread 1/6 of the mixture on each noodle. Roll up the 6 noodles and place them in the toaster oven pan. Spoon tomato sauce over stuffed noodles. Sprinkle with remaining Parmesan cheese and basil. Cover with a sheet of foil. Bake in a preheated 350° toaster oven for 45 minutes. Remove foil and bake for an additional 15 minutes. Serve warm.

CRISPY LOW-FAT EGGPLANT

This mouth-watering recipe is a treat from Carolyn Keefe, a health-conscious and talented cook. She serves it warm over fresh linguine with a spicy tomato sauce.

1 cup breadcrumbs
2 tbs. Parmesan cheese
1 cup nonfat plain or vanilla yogurt
1 small eggplant
ice cold water
3 tbs. vegetable oil

In a shallow bowl, combine breadcrumbs and Parmesan cheese. Mix well. Place yogurt in another bowl. Wash eggplant, but do not peel. Cut eggplant into $\frac{1}{4}$-inch to $\frac{1}{2}$-inch rounds. Place eggplant slices in a bowl of ice cold water for 10 minutes. Dip eggplant in yogurt, generously covering all sides. Dredge yogurt-covered eggplant slices with breadcrumb mixture and shake off excess. Place eggplant slices on a lightly oiled toaster oven pan or baking sheet. Bake in a preheated 350° toaster oven for 20 minutes. Turn occasionally. Remove from oven and set aside. Repeat until all slices are cooked.

MEXICAN SALSA-STUFFED POTATOES

Servings: 2

Here's a vegetarian treatment for baked potatoes — looks great, tastes great and is low in fat. The salsa comes together perfectly, and if you plant your own vegetable garden, it's a great way to make use of all those extra tomatoes. We like to make a large batch and serve it with nachos or tortilla chips. For variety, spread a thin layer of the salsa over a fish fillet or chicken breast before baking.

2 large baking potatoes
1/2 large tomato, cut into small chunks
1/2 large tomato, pureed
1 tbs. olive oil
1/2 small red onion, finely chopped

1/2 large red bell pepper, diced
1 clove garlic, thinly sliced
1/2 tsp. chili powder
1/8 tsp. ground cumin
1 tbs. chopped fresh cilantro

Carefully scrub potatoes with a vegetable brush under cold running water to remove dirt. Pierce potatoes and place directly on the toaster oven rack. Bake in a preheated 450° toaster oven for 50 to 55 minutes. In a medium bowl, combine remaining ingredients and mix well. When potatoes are done cooking, slice in half lengthwise. Spread a thick layer of salsa on potato halves. Bake in a preheated 375° toaster oven for 14 minutes. Serve immediately.

CAULIFLOWER-BROCCOLI CHEESE CASSEROLE

Servings: 2

Here's an innovative, steamy casserole with enough flavor to satisfy everyone.

11/2 cups cauliflower florets
1 cup chopped broccoli florets and stems,
   chopped into 1-inch pieces
1 tsp. olive oil
1 small red onion, finely chopped
10 oz. fat-free ricotta cheese

2 eggs
2 tbs. all-purpose flour
1/4 tsp. salt
1/4 tsp. pepper
1/8 tsp. chili powder
2 tbs. grated Parmesan cheese

Steam cauliflower and broccoli for 2 minutes and set aside. Heat olive oil in a skillet and sauté red onion over medium heat for 3 to 4 minutes, or until soft. In a medium bowl, mix together ricotta cheese and eggs. Stir flour, salt and pepper into cheese-egg mixture. Add broccoli and red onion. Stir well. Pour into 2 ungreased oval 4½-x-7-inch ovenproof casseroles. Sprinkle top with chili powder and Parmesan cheese. Bake in a preheated 375° toaster oven for 35 to 40 minutes.

TOMATOES WITH WHITE WINE AND HERBS

Servings: 2

Growing your own herbs is fun and easy, and the flavor rewards are large. Whenever possible, use fresh herbs in your cooking: just triple the quantity of dried herbs called for. Fresh farm-stand quality tomatoes work best here. Serve with seafood or chicken.

3 medium tomatoes
1 tsp. vegetable oil
2 tbs. white wine
2 tbs. seasoned breadcrumbs
2 tbs. crumbled feta cheese
1 tsp. dried basil
1 tsp. dried oregano
1/2 tsp. pepper

Slice tomatoes in half. Coat the toaster oven pan with vegetable oil. Place tomato halves on pan, cut side up. Drizzle tomato halves with white wine and sprinkle with a thin layer of breadcrumbs. Top breadcrumbs with feta cheese and sprinkle with herbs and pepper. Bake in a preheated 350° toaster oven for 25 minutes. Serve warm.

BAKED BEETS

Beets are a neglected vegetable full of nutritional goodies, like vitamin C, vitamin A and potassium. Add them to your menus for variety. This recipe gives them a little flavor zing, and baking helps to retain their flavor, color and vitamins.

3/4 lb. fresh beets, about 2-inch diameter
water
2 tbs. butter, melted

1 tsp. grated fresh orange peel (zest)
1/4 tsp. grated ginger root
1/4 tsp. dried parsley, or 1 tsp. fresh

Remove stems from beets and poke them with a fork. Pour 1/4-inch water into the toaster oven pan. Place the drip tray on pan, over water, in the lower position. Arrange beets on tray. Bake in a preheated 350° toaster oven for 1 1/2 hours. Remove skins and slice cooked beets. Mix with butter, orange zest, ginger root and parsley.

VARIATION

Dice peeled, cooked beets and combine with an equal quantity of diced raw apples. Toss with *Basic Balsamic Vinaigrette,* page 65. Refrigerate to chill. Serve as a refreshing salad or cold side dish.

BASIC BALSAMIC VINAIGRETTE

Makes: about 1 cup

Use these dressings as a sauce for cooked or raw vegetables, a marinade for seafood and meats, and over salads and deli-style sandwiches. The second recipe is a bit more luxurious and should be used immediately for maximum flavor.

3 tbs. balsamic vinegar
3/4 cup olive oil
1/4 tsp. pepper

2 tsp. chopped fresh basil, or 1/2 tsp. dried
2 cloves garlic, minced or pressed
1 tbs. fresh lemon juice

In a medium bowl, whisk ingredients together until evenly blended.

HONEY-MUSTARD BALSAMIC VINAIGRETTE

Makes: 3/4 cup

1 1/2 tsp. honey
2 tbs. Dijon mustard
1/4 tsp. dry mustard
1/4 cup balsamic vinegar

1 tbs. fresh lemon juice
1/4 cup olive oil
1 tsp. maple syrup
1 clove garlic, minced or pressed

In a small bowl, whisk ingredients together.

CHICKEN ENTRÉES

BAKED STUFFED CHICKEN OASIS

Serve this delicious, elegant entrée with baked potatoes or rice and steamed vegetables. Remember, a chicken has 1 breast, and 2 breast halves!

2 boneless, skinless chicken breast halves
4 strips cooked bacon, limp not crisp
2 broccoli spears, about 4 inches long and
   $\frac{1}{2}$-inch thick
2 oz. Monterey Jack cheese, shredded
$\frac{1}{4}$ cup milk

$\frac{1}{4}$ cup breadcrumbs
1 tsp. butter
1 cup thinly sliced mushrooms
2 tbs. flour
$\frac{3}{4}$ cup chicken broth
$\frac{1}{4}$ tsp. dried basil

Rinse chicken and pat dry. Flatten each chicken breast half with a wooden or metal mallet. Lay 2 strips of bacon across each piece of chicken. Place 2 pieces of broccoli on top of bacon strips and cover with cheese. Roll each chicken piece tightly and secure with wooden picks. Dip rolled chicken into milk and coat with breadcrumbs. In a small pan, melt butter. Add mushrooms and sauté for 4 to 5 minutes. Add flour and mix well. Add chicken broth and basil. Bring to a boil, reduce heat and simmer for 5 minutes. Place each rolled chicken breast in a small oval ovenproof baking dish or place both in the toaster oven pan. Pour sauce over chicken and bake in a preheated 375° toaster oven for 30 minutes.

SPINACH SALAD WITH DRIED CRANBERRIES, TOASTED ALMONDS AND ROAST CHICKEN

Servings: 2

Serve this beautiful salad with the roasted chicken for a delicious and satisfying meal or omit the chicken and let the salad compliment your main dish.

2 boneless, skinless chicken breast halves
5 tbs. olive oil
½ tsp. thyme, dried
1 tbs. water
juice of half lemon
½ tsp. balsamic vinegar
½ tsp. sugar
salt and pepper to taste
4 cups baby spinach leaves, washed and dried
⅛ cup almond slices
⅛ cup dried cranberries
1 medium cucumber, peeled, sliced
2 large red-ripe tomatoes, cut in wedges or 1 cup small cherry tomatoes, cut in half
1 small red onion, sliced in thin rings

To create dressing and marinate, combine olive oil, thyme, water, lemon juice, vinegar, sugar, salt and pepper in a small bowl and mix well. Divide mixture in half and reserve half for marinate and half for the dressing. Place chicken with the marinate in a large zip top plastic bag. Refrigerate for at least one hour or overnight.

Preheat the toaster oven on broil for 5 minutes. Place chicken on a toaster oven pan and broil for 15 minutes on each side or until cooked through. Remove chicken from oven; let cool and slice into 1-inch strips. Place the almond slices on the toaster oven tray in a preheated 400° toaster oven for 3 to 5 minutes, or until lightly toasted. In a large bowl, combine spinach, cucumber, tomatoes and red onions. Toss well. Divide salad onto 2 small serving plates and top with toasted almonds, dried cranberries and chicken strips. Serve with reserved salad dressing.

CHICKEN AND BROCCOLI CASSEROLE

Serve this rich, delicious main course any time of the year with a fresh garden salad.

½ bunch broccoli (about 2 cups broccoli
   pieces)
1 tbs. butter
1 tbs. flour
¾ cup milk
salt and pepper to taste

½ cup shredded cheddar cheese
¼ cup shredded Monterey Jack cheese
2 boneless, skinless chicken breast halves,
   cut into 1-inch pieces
2 tbs. seasoned breadcrumbs

Cut broccoli in small ½-inch pieces and steam for 2 minutes; set aside. In a medium saucepan, melt butter, add flour and stir continuously until well blended. Add milk and stir until sauce thickens. Add salt and pepper. Remove from heat and mix in cheeses. Add chicken and broccoli. Stir until chicken and broccoli are evenly coated with sauce. Pour chicken mixture into two oval ungreased individual 4½-x-7-inch ovenproof casseroles. Sprinkle with breadcrumbs. Bake in a preheated 350° toaster oven for 45 minutes.

TOMATO-BASIL CHICKEN WITH NEW POTATOES

It takes only a few minutes to prepare this dish — which gives you plenty of time to set the table, prepare a nice green salad and work on dessert while the chicken is cooking.

2 boneless, skinless chicken breast halves
1 can (14.5 oz.) stewed tomatoes, diced, with juice
1 clove garlic, minced or pressed
$1/2$ tsp. dried basil
$1/8$ tsp. pepper
5-6 small new potatoes, cut into $1/4$-inch slices

Rinse chicken, pat dry and cut into 1-x-3-inch strips. In a large bowl, combine tomatoes, garlic, basil and pepper. Mix well. Add chicken and potatoes and mix well. Spread mixture on the toaster oven pan. Try not to overlap chicken pieces. Bake in a preheated 375° toaster oven for 60 minutes.

CRUSTLESS CHICKEN PIE

This recipe is easy to put together and is perfect for lunch or dinner. The flavors and texture are wonderful and it always gets rave reviews.

2 tbs. butter
1 tbs. flour
$1/8$ tsp. salt
$1/4$ tsp. pepper
$1/2$ tsp. dried thyme
$2/3$ cup chicken broth
2 boneless, skinless chicken breast halves,
    cut into $1/4$-inch strips

$1/2$ cup drained corn kernels, fresh or frozen
$1/2$ cup diced carrots
$1/2$ cup drained peas, fresh or frozen
$1/2$ cup shredded zucchini
3 potatoes, boiled or baked, mashed

Melt butter in a skillet and add flour, salt, pepper and thyme. Cook for 2 minutes and add chicken broth. Stir continuously and cook until sauce has thickened. Add chicken and cook for 7 minutes. Divide mixture in half and pour into two $5^1/2$-inch round, 2-inch deep ovenproof casseroles. In the following order, top chicken with corn, carrots, peas, zucchini and mashed potatoes. Bake in a preheated 375° toaster oven for 30 to 35 minutes.

SPICY CHICKEN BREAST

Servings: 2

The breadcrumb and cornmeal combination has been a well-kept secret for a low fat, crunchy texture. When combined with an assertive spicy flavor, this makes a winner that beats commercially prepared coatings by miles.

2 boneless, skinless chicken breast halves
3 tbs. breadcrumbs
2 tbs. cornmeal
1/4 tsp. chili powder
1/4 tsp. garlic powder
1/4 tsp. dried chervil

1/8 tsp. ground cumin
1/4 tsp. pepper
1 tsp. grated Parmesan cheese
1/3 cup milk
2 tsp. vegetable oil

Rinse chicken under cold running water and pat dry. In a shallow bowl, combine breadcrumbs, cornmeal, chili powder, garlic powder, chervil, cumin, pepper and Parmesan cheese. Mix well. Pour milk into another shallow dish and dip chicken in milk. Coat each side of chicken with breadcrumb-cornmeal mixture and shake off excess. Lightly oil the toaster oven pan with 1 tsp. of the vegetable oil. Place chicken on pan and drizzle with remaining oil. Bake in a preheated 400° toaster oven for 30 minutes.

ITALIAN-STYLE CHICKEN KABOBS

If you're in a big hurry, marinate the chicken in Italian salad dressing instead of this marinade. Wooden skewers should be soaked in water for about 20 minutes before using so they will not burn. Serve over steamed white rice, with fresh rolls.

MARINADE

3 tbs. balsamic vinegar
¾ cup olive oil
⅛ tsp. pepper
1 clove garlic, minced or pressed

¼ tsp. dried basil
¼ tsp. dried parsley
1 tbs. fresh lemon juice

Combine all ingredients in a bowl and whisk together until evenly blended.

KABOBS

2 boneless, skinless chicken breast halves
3 slices bacon
1 large red bell pepper

1 large red or white onion
1 large tomato
1 cup Marinade or Italian dressing

Rinse chicken, pat dry and cut into 1-inch cubes. Cut bacon slices into 1-inch pieces. Cut pepper into 1-inch pieces. Cut onion into quarters and separate layers. Cut tomato into small 1-inch wedges.

In a medium bowl, combine chicken with marinade and refrigerate for 2 to 4 hours. On each of six 10-inch skewers, alternately thread a cube of chicken, 3 pieces of bacon, and a piece of pepper, tomato and onion. Place the toaster oven drip tray in the upper position on the oven pan. Place skewers on the tray and broil for 18 to 20 minutes. Turn occasionally and brown top for 1 to 2 minutes.

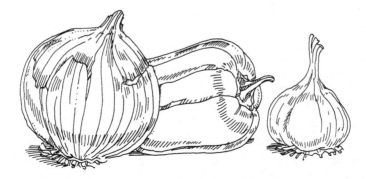

TOASTER OVEN-BARBECUED CHICKEN WINGS

Servings: 3-4

Next time, try chicken wings in a gusty sauce with a sensational flavor. It's good on drumsticks or other chicken parts.

2 tbs. olive oil
1/4 cup finely chopped onion
1/2 cup ketchup
2 tbs. Worcestershire sauce
1 tbs. white vinegar
1 tbs. fresh lemon juice
1/8 tsp. pepper
1/2 tsp. dry mustard
1 1/2 lb. chicken wings

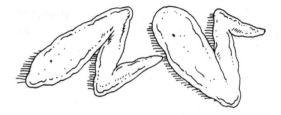

Heat oil in a medium saucepan. Add onion and sauté for 5 minutes. Add ketchup, Worcestershire sauce, vinegar, lemon juice, pepper and dry mustard. Simmer for 12 minutes. Cut chicken wings into 2 pieces at the joint, rinse and pat dry. Place chicken pieces on the toaster oven pan and coat liberally with 3/4 of the sauce. Bake in a preheated 450° toaster oven for 50 minutes. Baste occasionally with remaining sauce. Serve warm.

SWEET AND SOUR CHICKEN WITH BELL PEPPER

Steamed white rice goes exceptionally well with this Oriental-style dish.

2 boneless, skinless chicken breast halves
1 can (5½ oz.) pineapple chunks, with juice
1 tbs. flour
2 tbs. brown sugar
1 tbs. fresh lemon juice
1 tbs. red wine vinegar

1 tbs. honey
1 tbs. light soy sauce
½ small red or green bell pepper, sliced
 into matchstick strips
½ cup thinly sliced mushrooms

Rinse chicken and pat dry. Separate pineapple chunks from juice. In a medium bowl, combine flour, brown sugar, pineapple juice, lemon juice, vinegar, honey and soy sauce. Mix well. Coat chicken in sauce, covering all sides. Place chicken on the toaster oven pan in one layer. Distribute pepper strips, mushrooms and pineapple chunks on top of chicken. Pour remaining sauce over chicken and cover with foil. Bake in a preheated 350° toaster oven for 20 minutes. Remove foil and bake for an additional 15 minutes.

CHICKEN CAESAR SALAD

This salad makes a satisfying and abundant meal by itself, and looks beautiful besides. This version of Caesar dressing leaves out the coddled egg.

2 boneless, skinless chicken breast halves
2 tbs. olive oil
1 clove garlic, minced or pressed
½ tsp. dried basil
⅛ tsp. pepper
1 small or ½ large head romaine lettuce
Dressing, follows
½ cup *Baked Herb Croutons,* page 21
1 tbs. shredded Parmesan cheese

Rinse chicken, pat dry and cut into 1-inch cubes. To make marinade for chicken, in a small bowl, combine 2 tbs. olive oil, garlic, basil and pepper. Place chicken pieces in a shallow bowl, thoroughly coat with marinade and refrigerate for 2 hours. Place chicken cubes on the toaster oven drip tray, inverted in the upper position on the toaster oven pan, and broil for 9 minutes. Turn chicken over and broil for an additional 9 minutes. Brown top for 2 minutes and set aside.

Separate, wash and dry lettuce leaves. Tear lettuce into small pieces. Toss chicken and lettuce with dressing. Sprinkle with croutons and Parmesan cheese.

DRESSING
3 tbs. olive oil
1 clove garlic, minced or pressed
1 tbs. fresh lemon juice
$1/8$ tsp. pepper
$1/8$ tsp. salt

Combine ingredients and mix well.

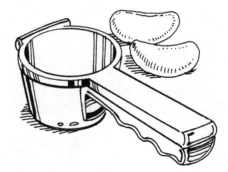

HEALTHY CHICKEN TARRAGON

Cooking with low fat or nonfat yogurt adds a special taste to cooked chicken or fish. This chicken is loaded with mouth-watering flavors. Serve it with potato and vegetables or on a lightly toasted bulky roll for a great-tasting sandwich.

2 boneless, skinless chicken breast halves
1 tbs. chopped fresh tarragon, or 1 tsp. dried
1/2 cup plain nonfat yogurt
2 tsp. fresh lemon juice
1 clove garlic, minced or pressed
1/8 tsp. salt
1/8 tsp. pepper
1 tsp. vegetable oil
1/4 cup shredded Monterey Jack cheese, optional

Rinse chicken and pat dry. In a shallow bowl, mix together tarragon, yogurt, lemon juice, garlic, salt and pepper. Set aside 2 tbs. of the yogurt mixture and add chicken to remaining yogurt mixture. Coat all sides of chicken, cover with plastic wrap and marinate in the refrigerator for 2 hours. Invert the toaster oven drip tray in the lower position and place the drip tray on the oven pan. Brush drip tray with vegetable oil. Place chicken on tray and broil for 10 minutes. Baste chicken occasionally with reserved 2 tbs. yogurt mixture. Turn chicken over and broil for an additional 10 minutes. Cover with cheese and broil for 2 minutes, or until cheese melts.

TOASTER OVEN-BAKED CHICKEN WITH CARROTS

An epicurean delight! This is the perfect meal for 1 or 2, and it's ideal for any size toaster oven. Excellent results every time.

2 boneless, skinless chicken breast halves
3 medium carrots, peeled, cut into 1-inch pieces
1 large potato, peeled, cut into 1-inch cubes
$1/2$ cup olive oil
$1/8$ tsp. pepper
1 dash salt
2 tbs. grated Parmesan cheese

Rinse chicken, pat dry and cut into 1-inch pieces. Combine all ingredients, except cheese, in a large bowl and mix thoroughly. Divide mixture into two 7-x-5-inch oval ovenproof baking dishes or the toaster oven pan. Sprinkle with Parmesan cheese. Bake in a preheated 350° toaster oven for 1 hour and 10 minutes. Serve hot.

GARLICKY LEMON PEPPER CHICKEN

Here's a good choice when you don't have much time to prepare the dish. The results are moist, flavorful, nourishing and attractive. Serve it with rice or pasta.

2 boneless, skinless chicken breast halves
1 tbs. olive oil
2 cloves garlic, minced or pressed
juice of $\frac{1}{2}$ lemon
$\frac{1}{2}$ tsp. pepper
$\frac{1}{2}$ tsp. dried basil

Rinse chicken and pat dry. In a small bowl, combine olive oil, garlic, lemon juice, pepper and basil. Mix well. Completely brush chicken with lemon-pepper mixture. Place chicken on the toaster oven pan and broil for 10 to 12 minutes. Turn chicken over and broil for an additional 10 to 12 minutes.

ROCK CORNISH GAME HENS
WITH PINEAPPLE AND HERBS

Here's an easy way to prepare a moist, flavorful and tender bird — perfect every time.

2 rock Cornish game hens, 1½ lb. each
1 tsp. olive oil
¼ tsp. dried thyme
¼ tsp. dried basil
⅛ tsp. pepper
1 can (5½ oz.) pineapple chunks, with juice

Remove necks and giblets from birds and discard, or reserve to use in gravy. Rinse birds very well and pat dry. Rub hens with olive oil. Place hens on the toaster oven pan. Do not let hens touch each other. Sprinkle with thyme, basil and pepper. Cover hens with pineapple chunks and drizzle with all the juice. Bake in a preheated 375° toaster oven for 1 hour and 15 minutes. Baste occasionally with pan juices. Place hens on warm individual serving plates and pour juices over birds.

CHICKEN TACOS DELUXE

This is a tasty recipe to serve to friends — fun to make and eat. For convenience, the entire cooking process is done in the toaster oven. Sour cream or guacamole can be added after the lettuce.

2 boneless, skinless chicken breast halves
2 tbs. fresh lemon juice
2 cloves garlic, minced or pressed
2 tsp. olive oil
1/4 tsp. dried basil
1/4 tsp. pepper
4 taco shells
1/2 cup diced tomatoes
1/4 cup salsa
1/2 cup shredded cheddar cheese
1 cup shredded lettuce

Rinse chicken, pat dry and cut into $1/4$-inch strips. To make marinade, combine lemon juice, garlic, olive oil, basil and pepper. Mix well. Add chicken to marinade in a medium bowl and refrigerate for 2 to 4 hours. Spread chicken on the toaster oven drip tray inverted in the oven pan in the upper position. Broil chicken on each side for 7 to 8 minutes. Spread cooked chicken in bottom of 4 taco shells. Cover chicken in the following order with diced tomatoes, salsa and cheese. Bake in a preheated 350° toaster oven for 4 to 5 minutes, or until cheese is melted. Top with shredded lettuce.

VARIATION

Fill the taco shells with cooked chicken and a combination of two or three of the following:

chopped green or red bell pepper
chopped black olives
refried beans
sliced jalapeño pepper
chopped green, red or yellow onion

CHICKEN BAKED IN A FRESH PARSLEY COAT

Servings: 2

Baking the chicken in a milk and herb coating creates a tender and irresistible chicken dish, and the cooking instructions are simple.

2 boneless, skinless chicken breast halves
1/4 cup milk
2 tbs. chopped fresh parsley
1/4 tsp. dried marjoram
1/4 tsp. garlic powder
1/4 tsp. dry mustard
1/8 tsp. salt
1/4 tsp. pepper
1 tbs. plus 1/2 tsp. olive oil
1 tbs. fresh lemon juice

Rinse chicken and pat dry. Pour milk into a shallow dish. In another shallow dish, combine parsley, marjoram, garlic, mustard, salt and pepper. Mix well. Dip chicken into milk, coating all sides. Coat both sides of chicken with parsley mixture. Brush the toaster oven pan with 1/2 tsp. olive oil. Place chicken breasts on pan. Drizzle with remaining olive oil and lemon juice. Bake in a preheated 350° toaster oven for 30 minutes.

FISH AND SHELLFISH ENTRÉES

BAKED HADDOCK WITH SHALLOTS

You can substitute just about any white fish for the haddock including tilapia, pollack, or flounder.

1 lb. haddock or cod fillets
juice of one lemon
$1/4$ cup shallots, minced
1 tbs. and 1 tsp. olive oil
$1/4$ cup seasoned breadcrumbs

In a small skillet, heat 1 tablespoon of olive oil over medium heat and add shallots. Sauté shallots for 3 to 4 minutes, or until shallots are translucent. Remove from heat and stir in breadcrumbs. Rinse fish under cold running water pat dry and drizzle with lemon. Line the toaster oven pan with aluminum foil and lightly brush pan with remaining olive oil. Place the fish in the toaster oven pan. Cover the fish with the shallot mixture and bake in a preheated 400° toaster oven for 20 to 25 minutes. Serve immediately with a fresh garden salad.

CRAB CAKES

For an attractive presentation, serve the crab cakes on a bed of lettuce with lemon wedges and tartar sauce.

1 lb. cooked crabmeat, shelled
1 1/2 cups seasoned breadcrumbs or cracker
   crumbs
1/2 cup finely chopped red bell pepper
1/4 cup minced shallots
1/4 cup light mayonnaise
2 tbs. Dijon mustard

1 1/2 tbs. fresh lemon juice
1/2 tsp. salt
1/2 tsp. ground cumin
1/8 tsp. ground red pepper
1/8 tsp. black pepper
2 large egg whites, beaten
2 tbs. olive oil

Combine the crabmeat, crumbs, red bell pepper, shallots, mayonnaise, mustard, lemon juice, salt, cumin, ground red pepper, black pepper and egg whites in a large bowl and mix well. Divide the mixture into 8 equal portions and shape into patties. Remove the toaster oven tray from the toaster oven and brush tray with olive oil. Preheat the toaster oven on broil for 5 minutes. Place the crab cakes on the toaster oven tray. Brush the tops of crab cakes with olive oil and broil for 7 minutes. Carefully flip the crab cakes. Brush crab cake tops with olive oil and broil for 7 more minutes. Serve warm.

LEMON PEPPER SALMON

Nonstick aluminum foil is available at most supermarkets and is great for a simple and easy cleanup when broiling fish in a toaster oven. This is a quick and easy preparation for salmon and the results are perfect!

2 salmon fillets, skinned (eight ounces each)
juice of $\frac{1}{2}$ lemon
$\frac{1}{2}$ tsp. ground black pepper

Rinse fish under cold running water and pat dry. Place the salmon in a toaster oven pan that has been lined with aluminum foil. Drizzle the fish with lemon juice and sprinkle evenly with pepper. Broil the fish for 8 minutes on each side or until desired degree of doneness. Serve immediately with lemon wedges.

CAJUN SHRIMP

For an eye-catching presentation serve this delicious combination over a bed of rice or alongside couscous.

1 lb. large shrimp, shelled and deveined
2 tbs. olive oil
1 tsp. paprika
$\frac{1}{4}$ tsp. crushed red pepper
$\frac{1}{4}$ tsp. chili power
$\frac{1}{4}$ tsp. dried oregano
$\frac{1}{4}$ tsp. dried basil
$\frac{1}{8}$ tsp. salt

Combine all ingredients in a large bowl. Mix and refrigerate for 1 hour. Transfer all ingredients to a toaster oven pan. Bake in a preheated 450° toaster oven for 5 minutes. Broil for an additional 3 to 5 minutes. Serve immediately

TUSCANY SHRIMP BAKE

Servings: 2

You can't go wrong with this recipe — a fabulous dish for anyone who enjoys fresh seafood and pasta.

$\frac{1}{2}$ lb. large shrimp, shelled and deveined
$\frac{1}{2}$ cup olive oil
2 cloves garlic, thinly sliced
1 tbs. fresh lemon juice
$\frac{1}{4}$ tsp. dried basil
$\frac{1}{2}$ tsp. dried parsley
cooked linguine, fettuccine or angel hair pasta, optional

Combine all ingredients, except pasta, in a large bowl. Mix and refrigerate for 8 hours or overnight. Transfer all ingredients to the toaster oven pan. Bake in a preheated 450° toaster oven for 5 minutes. Broil for an additional 3 minutes. Serve in small oval serving dishes or over hot pasta.

BAKED SOLE WITH TOASTED ALMONDS

This dish has a nice blend of flavors and is quick and easy to prepare. You can use this same recipe for red snapper or cod.

1 lb. sole fillets
1/4 cup slivered almonds
1 tbs. seasoned breadcrumbs
1/4 tsp. sweet paprika
1/2 tsp. fresh lemon juice
1/2 tsp. fresh lime juice
1 tbs. butter

Rinse fish under cold running water and pat dry. Toast slivered almonds in a dry skillet over medium heat, stirring constantly until golden brown. In a small bowl, combine breadcrumbs and paprika. Mix well. Coat oven pan lightly with vegetable spray. Place fish on pan and drizzle with lemon and lime juice. Sprinkle with breadcrumb mixture. Scatter slivered almonds on top of fish and dot with small pieces of butter. Bake in a preheated 400° toaster oven for 8 minutes, or until fish is opaque.

HERB-BAKED HALIBUT

Servings: 2

This treatment is equally delicious on other lean, mild-flavored fish.

1 lb. halibut fillets
$1/2$ cup plain nonfat yogurt
$1/4$ tsp. dried chervil
$1/8$ tsp. dried basil
$1/8$ tsp. dried parsley
$1/4$ cup shredded Monterey Jack cheese
1 tsp. olive oil
$1/8$ tsp. salt
$1/8$ tsp. pepper

Rinse fish under cold running water and pat dry. In a small bowl, combine yogurt, chervil, basil, parsley and cheese. Mix thoroughly and set aside. Lightly brush all sides of fish with olive oil. Place fish on the toaster oven pan or in 2 ovenproof oval baking dishes. Sprinkle with salt and pepper. Bake in a preheated 425° toaster oven for 15 to 18 minutes, or until fish is opaque. Spread yogurt mixture evenly on top of fish and bake for an additional 2 to 4 minutes, or until cheese melts.

SIMPLY LEMON THYME COD

Servings: 2

Be sure to select fresh, odorless fish that's free of bruises and brown spots. This recipe works with cod, scrod, haddock, pollack, hake, flounder and halibut.

1 lb. cod fillet
½ cup thinly sliced mushrooms
1 tbs. seasoned breadcrumbs
¼ tsp. dried thyme
juice of ½ lemon
1 tbs. butter
4 sprigs fresh parsley for garnish
4 lemon wedges

Rinse fish under cold running water and pat dry. Place fish on the toaster oven pan. Cover fish with a layer of mushrooms and top with breadcrumbs. Sprinkle with thyme and drizzle with lemon juice. Dot with small dabs of butter. Bake in a preheated 400° toaster oven for 15 minutes. Garnish with parsley sprigs and serve with lemon wedges.

DILLED SWORDFISH

The "top brown" control on your toaster oven allows you to create a restaurant-quality grilled flavor in the broiled fish. Occasionally fresh swordfish has an ocean scent which can be substantially reduced by increasing the marinading time. Serve with a fresh garden salad and warm rolls for a delicious and nutritious meal.

2 swordfish steaks,
   8 oz. each
2 tbs. olive oil
1/2 tsp. dried
   dill weed
juice of 1/2 lemon
2 tsp. butter

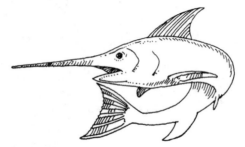

Rinse fish under cold running water and pat dry. To prepare marinade, combine olive oil, dill weed and lemon juice in a shallow dish. Place fish in marinade, coating each side. Refrigerate for 4 to 8 hours. Insert the toaster oven drip tray in the upper position. Place fish on drip tray. Broil fish for 6 to 8 minutes on each side. Dot top of fish with butter and "top brown" for 2 1/2 minutes.

TOASTER OVEN-FRIED FISH STICKS

This can be served as an appetizer, side dish or main course. You can substitute scrod, flounder or haddock fillets.

1 lb. cod fillets
$\frac{1}{2}$ cup milk
$\frac{1}{2}$ cup breadcrumbs
1 tsp. grated Parmesan cheese
$\frac{1}{8}$ tsp. pepper
$\frac{1}{8}$ tsp. salt
2 tbs. olive oil
4 lemon wedges
tartar sauce, ketchup or salsa, optional

Rinse fish under cold running water and pat dry. Cut fish into 1-x-3-inch strips. Pour milk in a shallow bowl. Combine breadcrumbs, Parmesan cheese, pepper and salt in another shallow bowl and mix well. Lightly oil the toaster oven pan. Coat all sides of fish with milk. Dredge fish with breadcrumb mixture and place in toaster oven pan. Carefully drizzle fish with remaining oil. Bake in a preheated 475° toaster oven for 15 to 17 minutes, or until golden brown. Serve with lemon wedges, and tartar sauce, ketchup or salsa if desired.

BAKED STRIPED BASS

The orange zest and garlic flavor the bass beautifully. You can substitute grouper or black sea bass or any firm-fleshed white fish.

1 lb. striped bass fillets
1/2 tsp. vegetable oil
1 tbs. fresh lemon juice
1 tsp. grated fresh orange peel (zest)
1/2 tsp. dried basil
1/8 tsp. salt
1/8 tsp. pepper
1 clove garlic, thinly sliced
2 tbs. dry white wine

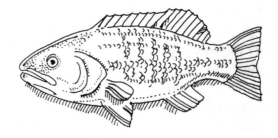

Rinse fish under cold running water and pat dry. Lightly oil the toaster oven pan. Place fish on pan and drizzle with lemon juice. Sprinkle fish with orange zest, basil, salt and pepper. Cover fish with a layer of garlic slices and drizzle with white wine. Cover with foil. Bake in a preheated 400° toaster oven for 15 to 18 minutes, or until fish is opaque.

BAKED SOLE WITH HERB SAUCE

The flavor of fresh herbs is perfectly balanced with the richness of the cheese sauce to make a delicious, elegant meal. You can substitute halibut, snapper or cod.

1 lb. sole fillets
1 tbs. olive oil
3/4 cup milk
1 tbs. butter
1 1/2 tbs. flour

3 tbs. shredded Monterey Jack or fontina cheese
1 tbs. chopped fresh parsley or basil

Rinse fish under cold running water and pat dry. Coat all sides of fish with olive oil and place in the toaster oven pan. Bake in a preheated 400° toaster oven for 8 minutes, or until fish is opaque.

While fish is baking, prepare herb sauce. Warm milk over low heat in a small saucepan. Melt butter in a medium saucepan. Over low heat, combine flour with melted butter, stirring continuously. Set heat to medium and slowly add milk. Continue to stir for 5 minutes, or until sauce begins to thicken. Slowly add shredded cheese and fresh herbs. Remove from heat when cheese is melted and pour over cooked fish. Serve immediately.

BAKED SCALLOPS

This popular dish goes over very well any time of the year. The sweet flavor of the scallops tastes great with toaster oven-roasted potatoes and a crisp garden salad.

1 lb. scallops
3 tbs. low fat or nonfat plain yogurt
1 egg white
1/4 tsp. pepper
1/3 cup cornmeal
1/3 cup seasoned breadcrumbs

1/2 tsp. paprika
1 tsp. grated Parmesan cheese
1/2 tsp. vegetable oil
2 tbs. butter or margarine, melted
6 lemon wedges

Rinse scallops and pat dry. In a small bowl, combine yogurt, egg white and pepper. Mix well. In a shallow bowl, combine cornmeal, breadcrumbs, paprika and Parmesan cheese. Mix well. Dip scallops in yogurt-egg mixture. Coat each scallop in breadcrumb mixture and shake off excess. Lightly coat the toaster oven pan with vegetable oil. Place scallops on pan and drizzle with butter. Bake in a preheated 375° toaster oven for 18 minutes. Serve with lemon wedges.

SEAFOOD CASSEROLE

Serve with freshly cooked fettuccine tossed with a good-quality olive oil.

1 tsp. vegetable oil
3 tbs. breadcrumbs
1 tbs. butter, melted
1 clove garlic, minced or pressed
1 lb. haddock or cod fillets
1/4 lb. small sea scallops

4 large shrimp, shelled and deveined
1/4 cup drained corn, fresh or canned
3 tbs. diced scallions
1 tbs. fresh lemon juice
1/4 tsp. dried basil
1 tbs. grated Parmesan cheese

Lightly coat the toaster oven pan with vegetable oil. In a small bowl, combine breadcrumbs, butter and garlic. Mix thoroughly and set aside. Rinse fish and scallops under cold running water and pat dry. Place fish, scallops, shrimp, corn and scallions in toaster oven pan or 2 small ovenproof casseroles. Drizzle with lemon juice. Sprinkle with basil and Parmesan cheese. Top with a layer of breadcrumb mixture. Bake in a preheated 425° toaster oven for 12 to 15 minutes.

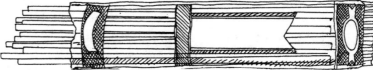

POLYNESIAN CATFISH

You can substitute haddock, cod or flounder for the catfish. Toasting the sesame seeds brings out their distinct flavor.

1 lb. catfish
2 tbs. soy sauce
1 clove garlic, minced or
   pressed
1 tsp. sesame seeds
1 tbs. chopped fresh
   cilantro
4 lemon wedges

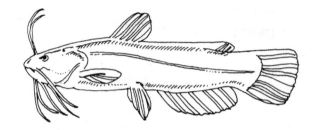

Rinse fish under cold running water and pat dry. In a small bowl, combine soy sauce with garlic. Toast sesame seeds in a dry skillet over medium heat, stirring constantly, until seeds are golden brown. Place fish on the toaster oven pan. Brush fish with all of the soy sauce mixture. Sprinkle with sesame seeds, cover and refrigerate for 1 hour. Bake in a preheated 400° toaster oven for 15 to 18 minutes, or until fish is opaque. Sprinkle fresh cilantro over cooked fish and serve immediately with lemon wedges.

LEMON DILL SNAPPER

This treatment for fish produces a healthy and delicious light entrée. You may substitute halibut, sole, orange roughy or grouper.

1 lb. red snapper
½ cup breadcrumbs
1 tsp. grated fresh lemon peel (zest)
1 tsp. dried dill weed
¼ tsp. paprika
¼ tsp. dried chervil

½ cup milk
1 tsp. vegetable oil
1 tbs. butter
4 lemon wedges
2 sprigs fresh basil for garnish

Rinse fish under cold running water and pat dry. In a shallow bowl, mix together breadcrumbs, lemon zest, dill weed, paprika and chervil. Pour milk in another shallow bowl and coat all sides of fish with milk. Dredge fish with lemon-dill mixture and place in a lightly oiled toaster oven pan. Dot with butter. Bake in a preheated 400° toaster oven for 10 to 12 minutes, or until fish is opaque. Serve with lemon wedges and garnish with fresh sprigs of basil.

BAKED TROUT ITALIANO

Servings: 2

This dish has a festive appearance and goes well with a bowl of fresh pasta cooked "al dente." You can substitute mackerel or bluefish.

1 lb. trout fillets
1 can (14.5 oz.) stewed tomatoes, diced,
  with juice
2 tbs. olive oil
2 cloves garlic, minced or pressed
1/4 lb. mushrooms, thinly sliced
1/4 cup sliced black olives
1/2 tsp. dried basil

1/2 tsp. dried marjoram
1/8 tsp. salt
1/8 tsp. pepper
4 tbs. breadcrumbs
1 tbs. lemon juice
1 tbs. grated Parmesan cheese
4 lemon wedges

Rinse fish under cold running water and pat dry. In a large bowl, combine tomatoes, 1 tbs. of the olive oil, garlic, mushrooms, olives, basil, marjoram, salt and pepper. Mix well. Brush toaster oven pan with remaining 1 tbs. olive oil. Sprinkle 2 tbs. of the breadcrumbs over oil. Place fish over breadcrumbs and drizzle with fresh lemon juice. Cover fish with tomato mixture and sprinkle with remaining breadcrumbs and Parmesan cheese. Bake in a preheated 375° toaster oven for 20 to 25 minutes. Serve immediately with lemon wedges.

CAJUN CATFISH

Store unused seasoning in an airtight container and use it sparingly on any fish or chicken.

1 lb. catfish fillets
Cajun Seasoning, follows
1 tsp. vegetable oil

1 tsp. chopped fresh basil
4 lemon wedges

Rinse fish under cold running water and pat dry. Lightly sprinkle all sides of fish with Cajun Seasoning. Lightly oil the toaster oven pan with vegetable oil. Place fish on pan and bake in a preheated 400° toaster oven for 8 to 10 minutes, or until fish is just opaque. Sprinkle with fresh basil. Serve with lemon wedges.

CAJUN SEASONING

2 tsp. paprika
$\frac{1}{2}$ tsp. cayenne pepper
$\frac{1}{2}$ tsp. garlic powder
$\frac{1}{2}$ tsp. pepper

$\frac{1}{2}$ tsp. dried oregano
$\frac{1}{2}$ tsp. dried thyme
$\frac{1}{2}$ tsp. chili powder

Combine all seasoning ingredients in a shallow bowl and mix thoroughly.

MEAT ENTRÉES

TERIYAKI LONDON BROIL

Serve with fresh vegetables and save the leftover steak for flavorful sandwiches. The light soy sauce reduces the sodium, but you can use regular soy sauce if you wish.

1/4 cup light soy sauce
1/4 cup vegetable oil
1/8 cup red wine
1 clove garlic, minced or pressed
1 tbs. diced onion
1 tbs. sugar
1 lb. London broil or flank steak
1 tsp. vegetable oil

In a shallow bowl, combine soy sauce, 1/4 cup oil, red wine, garlic, onion and sugar. Place steak in sauce, coat thoroughly and marinate in the refrigerator for 2 to 4 hours. Turn steak over occasionally. Set the toaster oven drip tray in the upper position on the toaster oven pan. Lightly coat drip tray with 1 tsp. vegetable oil. Place pan in oven and broil steak for 10 to 12 minutes on each side. To serve, carve meat diagonally across the grain into thin slices.

NEW YORK SIRLOIN WITH HERB BUTTER

Servings: 2

Herb butter adds a nice flavor to the beef. Try the butter on chicken, fish, vegetables or bread. We give instructions for cooking the beef medium-done, but warn you of the health risk from underdone beef. On an instant-read thermometer, 140° is rare, 170° is well done.

1½ tbs. butter, softened
1 clove garlic, minced or pressed
¼ tsp. dried basil
¼ tsp. dried oregano

⅛ tsp. pepper
½ tsp. olive oil
2 New York sirloin steaks, 12 oz. each

To prepare herb butter, combine softened butter, garlic, basil, oregano and pepper in a small bowl and blend together with a fork or spoon. Keep refrigerated until ready to use. Place the toaster oven drip tray in the upper position on the toaster oven pan. Brush olive oil on both sides of steak. Place meat on tray. Broil for 12 to 14 minutes on each side for medium. Cooking time may vary depending on the thickness and temperature of the meat*. Cut into steak to test. Remove from oven. Place steak on a warm serving platter and top each steak with ½ of the herb butter. Serve immediately.

Health authorities discourage eating undercooked beef because of possible bacterial contamination.

GREAT HAMBURGERS

Serve with tomato slices, lettuce leaves, chopped onions and ketchup or mayonnaise on toasted buns.

1 lb. ground chuck
1 tbs. finely chopped red onion
2 tsp. Worcestershire sauce
$1/8$ tsp. salt
$1/8$ tsp. pepper
1 tsp. vegetable oil
4 sesame seed buns, toasted

In a large bowl combine beef, onions, Worcestershire sauce, salt and pepper. Mix gently and shape into 4 patties about $1/2$- to $3/4$-inch thick. Set the toaster oven drip tray on the toaster oven pan in the upper position. Lightly coat drip tray with vegetable oil. Place patties on tray and broil for 7 to 8 minutes on each side for medium*. Place each burger on bottom half of bun, cover with toppings of choice and cover with top half of bun.

Health authorities discourage eating undercooked beef because of possible bacterial contamination.

ITALIAN-STYLE MEAT LOAF

Meat loaf is one of the twelve most popular foods in America. You'll receive lots of raves on this version. Slice leftover meat loaf for sandwiches. This recipe fits nicely into two small 6-x-3$\frac{1}{2}$-x-2-inch loaf pans or one large 8$\frac{1}{2}$-x-4$\frac{1}{2}$-x-2$\frac{1}{2}$-inch loaf pan.

1 lb. ground beef	$\frac{1}{2}$ tsp. dry mustard
1 cup breadcrumbs	$\frac{1}{3}$ cup red wine
1 small onion, minced	$\frac{1}{4}$ tsp. dried basil
1 clove garlic, minced or pressed	$\frac{1}{4}$ tsp. pepper
1 egg, beaten	$\frac{1}{4}$ tsp. salt
$\frac{1}{4}$ cup grated Parmesan cheese	2 slices bacon, uncooked

In a large bowl, combine all ingredients except bacon. Mix thoroughly with your hands. Pat meat mixture evenly into 2 individual loaf pans (or a large loaf pan, if you prefer). Cut bacon strips in half and place on top of meat loaf. Bake in a preheated 350° toaster oven for 45 minutes. Serve warm.

VARIATION

Pour warm *Italian Plum Tomato Sauce,* page 135, over cooked meat loaf slices before serving.

SUPER CHILI CHEESEBURGERS

Vibrantly flavored, these cheeseburgers are perfect when you're in the mood for something spicy. Use Picante Salsa, page 31, or your favorite commercial variety. Add your usual hamburger favorites, such as tomato slices, lettuce or onion.

1 lb. ground chuck or ground round
1/4 cup *Picante Salsa,* page 31
1 tsp. finely chopped onion
2 tbs. breadcrumbs
1 clove garlic, minced or pressed
1/4 tsp. dried basil

1/8 tsp. salt
1/8 tsp. pepper
1 tsp. vegetable oil
4 slices cheddar cheese
4 hamburger buns, toasted

In a large bowl, combine beef, salsa, onion, breadcrumbs, garlic, basil, salt and pepper. Mix gently and shape into 4 patties about 1/2- to 3/4-inch thick. Set the toaster oven drip tray on the toaster oven pan. Lightly coat tray with vegetable oil. Place patties on tray and broil for 7 to 8 minutes on each side for medium*. Place a slice of cheddar cheese on each patty and cook for 1 more minute. Serve on toasted buns with your favorite toppings.

*Health authorities discourage eating undercooked beef because of possible bacterial contamination.

BROILED MARINATED FLANK STEAK

Servings: 3

In addition to serving this flavorful meat with a side dish and a salad, arrange slices of beef on lightly toasted bread with cuts of tomato, chopped onion, lettuce and mayonnaise for great sandwiches.

¼ cup balsamic vinegar
2 tbs. olive oil
2 tbs. honey
¼ tsp. dried sage
¼ tsp. dried oregano

¼ tsp. pepper
⅛ tsp. salt
1 lb. flank steak
1 tsp. vegetable oil

In a shallow bowl, combine vinegar, olive oil, honey, sage, oregano, pepper and salt. Mix well. Place steak in marinade, coating both sides. Marinate in the refrigerator for 4 hours or overnight. Turn steak over occasionally. Set the toaster oven drip tray in the upper position on the toaster oven pan. Lightly coat drip tray with vegetable oil. Place pan in the toaster oven and broil steak for 10 to 12 minutes on each side. To serve, cut into thin slices across the grain at a slanted angle.

BROILED LAMB CHOPS

Lamb chops are a special treat, and these are brimming with flavor. This beautiful presentation for lamb goes especially well with baked potatoes.

2 rib or loin lamb chops, about 1¼-inch thick
⅛ cup red wine
1 tbs. olive oil
2 cloves garlic, minced or pressed
¼ tsp. dried mint
⅛ tsp. dried rosemary
⅛ tsp. dried oregano
⅛ tsp. pepper

Trim excess fat from lamb chops. In a shallow dish, combine wine, oil, garlic, mint, rosemary and oregano. Mix well. Place chops in marinade, coating all sides. Cover and refrigerate for 4 hours or overnight. Insert the toaster oven drip tray in the upper position and place the toaster oven drip tray on the oven pan. Place chops on the tray and broil on each side for 6 to 7 minutes. Baste occasionally with remaining marinade. Use tongs to turn meat over; do not pierce with a fork. Broil until chops are done to your desire. Season with pepper and serve immediately.

PORK MEDALLIONS IN PECAN COATS

Servings: 2

This is an exotic preparation for pork. These pork medallions are so beautiful and delicious you'll want to serve them at your next elegant dinner party. Serve with Tomatoes With White Wine and Herbs, *page 63, baked potatoes and a salad.*

2 tbs. finely chopped pecans
1/4 cup seasoned breadcrumbs
1/4 tsp. pepper
1/4 cup soy sauce
1 tbs. fresh lemon juice

1 clove garlic, minced or pressed
1 tbs. brown sugar
1/2 lb. pork loin, cut into 3/4-inch-thick slices
1 tsp. vegetable oil

In a shallow bowl, combine pecans, breadcrumbs and pepper. Mix thoroughly and set aside. In another shallow bowl, combine soy sauce, lemon juice, garlic and brown sugar. Mix well and marinate pork in mixture for 1 hour, turning occasionally. Coat pork medallions with pecan mixture and shake off excess. Lightly coat the toaster oven pan with 1/2 tsp. vegetable oil. Place pork medallions on the pan and drizzle with remaining 1/2 tsp. vegetable oil. Bake in a preheated 425° toaster oven for 20 minutes.

ZESTY PORK CHOPS

Servings: 2

This is a tasty and moist preparation for pork chops. Use an instant-read thermometer to test the temperature of the cooked meat. It should read 160°. Serve with mashed potatoes.

juice of ½ lime
1 clove garlic, minced or pressed
¼ cup dry white wine
1 small onion, chopped
2 tbs. chopped fresh parsley
½ tsp. chili powder
½ tsp. sugar
⅛ tsp. cayenne pepper
⅛ tsp. salt
2 pork loin chops, 1-inch thick

Combine all ingredients, except pork chops, in a blender or food processor. Process for 1 to 2 minutes, or until smooth. Trim off excess fat from pork chops. In a shallow bowl, combine pork chops with lime mixture. Cover and refrigerate for 6 hours or overnight. Place pork chops on the toaster oven pan and pour marinade over chops. Bake in a preheated 375° toaster oven for 30 minutes.

BAKED PORK CHOPS WITH FENNEL

This is an unusual combination of flavors for pork chops, but we think you'll like the results.

2 tbs. butter
1 small red onion, coarsely
   chopped
1 cup thinly sliced mushrooms
3 slices prosciutto, diced
2 pork chops, ½- to ¾-inch
   thick
½ tsp. fennel seeds

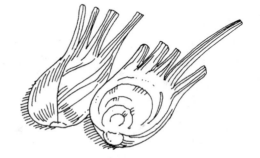

Melt butter in a nonstick skillet. Add onion and sauté over medium heat for 2 to 3 minutes. Add mushrooms and prosciutto; sauté for 2 to 3 minutes. Place pork chops on the toaster oven pan. Spread sautéed mixture over pork chops and sprinkle with fennel seeds. Bake in a preheated 375° toaster oven for 25 to 27 minutes. To test, insert an instant-read meat thermometer in the chops: it should read 160°.

HERB-BAKED PORK CHOPS

This toaster oven special for "the other white meat" is quick and easy to prepare. These chops go well with steamed spinach and sweet potatoes.

1/4 cup breadcrumbs
1/8 tsp. garlic powder
1/4 tsp. paprika
1/4 tsp. dried rosemary
1/4 tsp. dried oregano
1/2 tsp. dried basil
1/4 tsp. pepper
1/4 tsp. grated Parmesan cheese
2 tsp. olive oil
2 pork chops, 1/2- to 3/4-inch thick

In a shallow dish, combine breadcrumbs, garlic powder, paprika, rosemary, oregano, basil, pepper and Parmesan cheese. Mix well. Brush olive oil on both sides of pork chops. Coat chops with breadcrumb mixture and shake off excess. Lightly coat the toaster oven pan with nonstick vegetable spray. Place chops on pan and bake in a preheated 425° toaster oven for 20 minutes.

SAVORY PORK CHOPS

Pork chops are really suited to cooking in a toaster oven, which is why we've included several pork chop recipes in our collection. Here's a new and exciting way to prepare them. If you can't find ground fennel seed, just grind the fennel seed with a mortar and pestle or in a spice mill. Try these chops served with Roasted Red-Skinned Potatoes, *page 53, and steamed broccoli.*

1 tbs. olive oil
2 tbs. fresh lemon juice
1 clove garlic, minced or pressed
$1/2$ tsp. fennel seeds, ground
2 pork chops, $1/2$- to $3/4$-inch thick

In a shallow dish, combine olive oil, lemon juice, garlic and fennel. Mix well. Coat chops with marinade and refrigerate for 2 hours. Insert the toaster oven drip tray in the lower position on the toaster oven pan. Place chops on tray and broil for 7 to 8 minutes on each side. An instant-read meat thermometer inserted into chops should read 160°.

HAWAIIAN KABOBS

You get a little touch of paradise with this colorful, sweet combination. Serve it with white rice and a crisp green salad. Use 10-inch skewers, and don't forget to presoak wooden ones for at least 20 minutes.

$\frac{1}{2}$ lb. sweet sausage, cut into 1-inch pieces
1 cup fresh pineapple chunks, in 1-inch pieces
$\frac{1}{2}$ medium-sized red bell pepper, cut into 1-inch squares
$\frac{1}{2}$ peach, cut into 1-inch pieces

$\frac{1}{2}$ tsp. grated fresh lime peel (zest)
1 tbs. fresh lemon juice
2 tbs. pineapple juice
1 tbs. olive oil
1 tsp. chopped fresh basil or parsley for garnish, optional

In a large bowl, combine sausage, pineapple, pepper squares, peach pieces, lime zest, lemon juice, pineapple juice and olive oil. Mix thoroughly. Cover with plastic wrap and refrigerate for at least 2 hours. Alternately thread sausage, pineapple, peppers and peaches onto 6 metal or presoaked bamboo skewers. Place the toaster oven drip tray in the upper position onto the toaster oven pan and lightly coat with vegetable spray. Broil for 20 to 25 minutes. Turn and brush with remaining marinade occasionally. Remove from oven and sprinkle with fresh herbs if desired.

ITALIAN SAUSAGE BAKE

Here is a recipe with a full palette of colors that is easy to prepare and really good. Serve it with warm crusty Italian bread and a crisp green salad.

½ lb. sweet Italian sausage
1 large potato
½ medium onion
½ green bell pepper
½ red bell pepper
1 tsp. olive oil
¼ tsp. dried oregano
¼ tsp. dried basil
⅛ tsp. salt
⅛ tsp. pepper

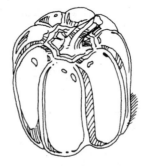

Cut sausage into 1-inch pieces and puncture with a fork. Peel and cut potato into ¾-inch cubes. Slice and separate onion and cut peppers into ½-inch strips. Arrange sausage, potatoes, onion and peppers in the toaster oven pan. Do not overlap sausage pieces. Drizzle with olive oil and sprinkle with oregano, basil and pepper. Bake in a preheated 375° toaster oven for 55 minutes. Turn occasionally.

SOUTH-OF-THE-BORDER FRANKS

These spicy dogs have an outdoor grilled flavor. Top them with Picante Salsa, *page 31, or use your favorite commercial brand. Cut the recipe in half for 2 servings. To add a little "heat," sprinkle cheese with red pepper flakes.*

4 frankfurter buns
4 frankfurters
1 tsp. vegetable oil
1 cup salsa
1 cup shredded Monterey Jack cheese

Lightly toast buns in the toaster oven and set aside. Place the toaster oven drip tray in the upper position on the toaster oven pan. Lightly coat tray with nonstick vegetable spray. Make 1/8-inch-deep slits diagonally across frankfurters about 2 inches apart and brush with vegetable oil. Place frankfurters on tray and broil for 8 minutes. Turn occasionally. Place frankfurters in toasted buns. Top with a layer of salsa, cover with cheese and place on pan. Bake in a preheated 350° toaster oven for 7 minutes, or until cheese melts. Serve immediately.

HOT SANDWICHES

HOT ANTIPASTO SANDWICH

Pine nuts, also known as pignolia, are available in the spice section of your supermarket. Sometimes you can find them available in bulk, for less money, in the produce section. To toast your own, spread a layer of nuts on the toaster oven pan and bake at 400° for 2 minutes.

1 tbs. olive oil
2 tsp. balsamic vinegar
1/4 tsp. dried basil
1/4 tsp. red pepper flakes
1 tbs. pine nuts, toasted
1 tbs. chopped sun-dried tomatoes, packed
  in oil or reconstituted
1/4 tsp. pepper

2 French rolls
8 thin slices prosciutto
4 slices Genoa salami
6 roasted red bell pepper strips, chopped,
  about 2 tbs.
6 slices tomato
2 slices provolone cheese

In a small bowl, combine olive oil, vinegar, basil, red pepper flakes, pine nuts, sun-dried tomatoes and pepper. Slice rolls in half lengthwise and toast in the toaster oven. Spread oil and vinegar mixture on 2 roll halves. Cover, in the following order, with 1/2 of the prosciutto, salami, roasted peppers, tomato slices and provolone cheese. Bake in a preheated 350° toaster oven for 10 minutes, or until cheese melts. Remove from oven, cover with remaining toasted halves and serve warm.

CHEESE STEAK SANDWICH

Servings:2

This is our version of the all-time favorite Philadelphia cheese steak sandwich; it comes out just right in the toaster oven. If you can get lemon-flavored black peppercorns, they add the perfect touch. If not, add a generous grind or two of regular black pepper. Serve it with chips or a salad.

½ lb. sirloin steak
¼ cup light Italian dressing
2 French rolls

freshly ground lemon-flavored black pepper
½ cup shredded low fat smoked mozzarella
or low fat smoked cheddar cheese

Cut steak into ¼-inch-thick strips. In a shallow bowl, combine steak strips with Italian dressing. Marinate in the refrigerator for at least 2 hours. Invert the toaster oven drip tray in the upper position and place drip tray on the toaster oven pan. Place steak strips on tray. Allow at least 1 inch between steak and heating element. Broil steak for 6 to 8 minutes on each side. Split rolls open, leaving top connected to bottom, and toast lightly. With rolls open, spread meat on both sides, season with pepper and top with cheese. Bake in a preheated 350° toaster oven for 12 to 15 minutes, or until cheese is melted. Serve open-faced or closed.

AS YOU LIKE IT SANDWICH

Servings: 2

You can't go wrong with this improvised sandwich. Use your imagination and play with the combinations. In place of the salami, try mortadella or bologna. And in place of the Swiss cheese, try cheddar, fontina, American or Gorgonzola.

8 slices summer squash, 1/8-inch-thick
    rounds (zucchini, yellow crookneck or
    pattypan)
1/4 cup balsamic vinegar
4 slices pumpernickel, rye or white bread
2 tbs. mustard
4 slices salami

6–8 slices Danish ham or turkey breast
2 slices red onion, separated into rings
2 slices Swiss cheese
1/4 tsp. dried thyme, or 1 tsp. fresh
1/4 tsp. dried tarragon, or 1 tsp. fresh
1/8 tsp. pepper

In a small bowl, combine squash with vinegar and marinate for 2 hours. Lightly toast 4 slices of bread. Spread mustard on 2 slices. Cover mustard with salami, followed by squash, ham, onion, cheese and seasonings. Bake in a preheated 350° toaster oven for 10 to 12 minutes, or until cheese melts. Top with remaining slices of toasted bread. Cut each sandwich in half diagonally and serve warm.

MARINATED CHICKEN BREAST SANDWICH

Servings: 2

The chicken is moist and flavorful and makes a sandwich that everyone will enjoy.

2 boneless, skinless chicken breast halves
3 tbs. olive oil
juice of ½ lemon
1 tbs. dry sherry
1 tbs. dry white wine
1 clove garlic, minced or pressed
½ tsp. dried oregano

¼ tsp. pepper
⅓ cup cooked spinach, well drained
2 tbs. crumbled feta cheese
2 sandwich rolls, or 4 slices bread of choice
lettuce leaves, optional
tomato slices, optional

Rinse chicken and pat dry. Whisk together oil, lemon juice, sherry, wine, garlic, oregano and pepper. In a shallow dish, combine chicken with oil mixture and marinate in the refrigerator for 4 hours or overnight. Combine spinach with feta cheese and set aside. Invert the toaster oven drip tray in the upper position and place drip tray on the toaster oven pan. Place chicken breast on drip tray. Allow at least 1 inch between chicken and heating element. Broil chicken for 10 minutes on each side. Spread with spinach-cheese mixture and wrap in foil. Heat in a 350° toaster oven for 12 minutes. Serve on rolls or bread topped with lettuce and tomato slices if desired.

SMOKY CHEESE AND HAM SANDWICH

Inspired by our interest in spicy cuisine, this is one of our personal favorites. It's easy to put together, and full of zesty flavor.

4 slices rye or pumpernickel bread
8 thin slices ham
8 slices zucchini, ⅛-inch-thick rounds
2 jalapeño peppers, cut into ⅛-inch
   circles
2 tsp. chopped fresh cilantro
2 tbs. shredded smoked cheddar
   cheese

Lightly toast bread. Lay 2 slices on the toaster oven tray. Place 4 slices ham on each slice and cover with sliced zucchini. Cover zucchini with jalapeño peppers, cilantro and shredded cheese. Bake in a preheated 350° toaster oven for 10 to 12 minutes. Remove from oven and cover with remaining slices of bread. Slice each sandwich in half diagonally and serve warm.

WHOLE WHEAT CALZONES

The small area of the toaster oven produces heat so intense, it resembles the cooking qualities of a brick-lined pizza oven, thereby creating a professional-quality crust for the calzones. To further enhance the crust, try lining the oven rack with small baking tiles, which are available at many specialty gourmet shops.

DOUGH

1 pkg. active dry yeast
1 cup plus 1 tbs. warm water
1 tbs. sugar
2¼ cups all-purpose flour

1 cup whole wheat flour
½ tsp. salt
3 tbs. olive oil

In a small bowl, dissolve yeast in warm water and add sugar. Set aside for 5 minutes. In a large bowl, combine flours and salt. Mix well. Add yeast mixture and oil to flour. Stir together to form a ball. Place ball of dough on a floured surface and knead for 10 minutes. Place dough in a greased bowl and turn to coat with grease. Cover with a towel or plastic wrap and allow to rise for 1½ hours in a draft-free area. Punch down dough. Return dough to bowl and cover with a towel or plastic wrap. Let rise for 30 minutes. Punch down again and allow to rest for 10 minutes.

FILLING

1 tsp. olive oil
1 cup ricotta cheese (can be low fat)
¼ cup chopped black olives
4 medium plum tomatoes, cut into chunks
1 can (14 oz.) artichoke hearts packed in water, drained and quartered
¾ cup shredded fontina cheese
½ tsp. dried basil
⅛ tsp. pepper

Divide dough into 4 equal pieces and roll each piece into a 9-inch circle. Brush half of each circle with olive oil. Leaving a 1-inch border, spread ricotta cheese evenly on oiled halves. Cover ricotta with olives, tomato chunks and artichoke hearts. Cover with a layer of fontina cheese and sprinkle with basil and pepper. Bring uncovered half of dough over filling to form a half moon. Seal calzones by crimping edges of dough with your fingers. Place calzones on a lightly oiled toaster oven pan. Brush tops of calzones with olive oil. Bake in a preheated 400° toaster oven for 35 minutes. Allow to cool for 10 minutes before serving. Serve hot or cold.

VEGGIE POCKET

Even children, who sometimes shy away from vegetables, like this vegetarian sandwich.

1 cup broccoli florets
1 medium carrot, cut into $1/4$-inch strips
1 small zucchini, cut into $1/4$-inch rounds
$1/2$ large red bell pepper, cut into $1/4$-inch strips
1 small onion, thinly sliced, separated into rings
2 pita breads
juice of $1/2$ lemon
1 tbs. chopped fresh parsley
1 tsp. chopped fresh chives
chili powder to taste
8 slices tomato, $1/4$-inch thick
2 slices American cheese, optional

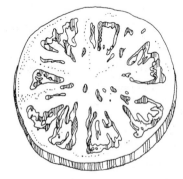

Parboil or steam broccoli, carrot, zucchini, pepper and onion. Cut pita breads in half to make 4 pockets. Divide vegetables into pockets. Drizzle with lemon juice and sprinkle with seasonings. Top with tomato slices and cheese. Bake in a preheated 350° toaster oven for 10 minutes, or until cheese is melted. Serve warm.

FRENCH BREAD PIZZA

You can use any baked French loaf or prepare your own by following the recipe for Mini French Bread Loaves *on page 43. This recipe can easily be increased for larger servings.*

2 *Mini French Bread Loaves,* or ¹/₂ French
   bread baguette
³/₄ cup tomato pizza sauce
¹/₂ cup shredded Monterey Jack, mozzarella
   or cheddar cheese

¹/₄ cup chopped black olives
4 artichoke hearts, cut into large pieces
¹/₄ tsp. dried basil, or 1 tsp. chopped fresh
¹/₄ tsp. dried oregano

Slice French bread lengthwise in half. Spoon tomato pizza sauce evenly over bread, leaving a ¹/₂-inch border around outside edge. Distribute cheese, olives and artichoke hearts on sauce. Sprinkle with basil and oregano. Lightly coat the toaster oven pan with nonstick vegetable spray. Place pizza on pan and bake in a preheated 350° toaster oven for 18 to 20 minutes. Broil for 4 to 5 minutes, or until cheese bubbles.

VARIATION

Use *Pizza Dough,* page 12, roll or stretch into a shape that fits your toaster oven pan or a pizza pan, and cover with sauce and topping as directed. Bake in a preheated 475° toaster oven for 18 to 20 minutes. Add cooked, crumbled sausage if you wish.

HOT APPLE AND RAISIN SANDWICH

You will love this unusual, absolutely delightful sandwich. The flavors come together perfectly. Good served with chips and pickles.

4 slices pumpernickel bread
1 apple, peeled, cored and thinly sliced
1 tbs. chopped fresh chives or scallions
2 tbs. raisins
2 tbs. chopped walnuts
$\frac{1}{2}$ cup shredded cheddar cheese (can be low fat)

Lightly toast bread. Cover 2 pieces of bread with a layer of sliced apples and sprinkle chives or scallions over apple slices. Cover remaining 2 pieces of bread with raisins and chopped walnuts. Sprinkle all 4 pieces of bread with cheddar cheese. Place bread on the toaster oven pan and broil for 5 to 7 minutes, or until cheese bubbles. Put sandwiches together, cut each in half diagonally and serve warm.

VARIATION
Omit chives or scallions and sprinkle apples with $\frac{1}{4}$ tsp. dried mint or 4 fresh mint leaves, torn into small pieces.

ROAST BEEF FLORENTINE ROLL-UPS

A little bit of Italy, a little bit of Mexico, and a lot of hearty goodness. This is a good choice for a casual lunch, or double the recipe, slice into 1½-inch pieces and serve on a platter as an appetizer or hors d'oeuvre for your next buffet. Serve with tortilla chips and salsa or guacamole.

2 small flour or whole wheat tortillas
¼ cup tomato sauce
1 small clove garlic, very thinly sliced
4 slices roast beef
pinch salt

⅛ tsp. pepper
½ cup fresh or frozen spinach, cooked and
   well drained
2 slices provolone cheese
1 tsp. olive oil

Cover 2 tortillas with a layer of tomato sauce, leaving a ½-inch border around the edges. Arrange garlic slices on top of sauce. Top with a layer of roast beef and season with salt and pepper. Cover roast beef with a layer of spinach and top with a slice of cheese. Starting on one side, roll each tortilla tightly and secure with picks. Brush tortillas with oil and bake in a preheated 325° toaster oven for 15 minutes. Serve warm.

ULTIMATE CHICKEN CUTLET SANDWICH

Servings:' 1

Use Italian Plum Tomato Sauce, *page 135, or any other favorite.*

1 French roll, 7 inches long
1 clove garlic, cut in half
1 boneless, skinless chicken breast half
$1/4$ cup breadcrumbs
$1/2$ tsp. grated Parmesan cheese
$1/8$ tsp. dried basil

Slice roll in half lengthwise and lightly toast in the toaster oven. Rub crusty surface with garlic and set aside. Rinse chicken under cold running water and pat dry. Fillet breast into 3 thin cutlets. Tenderize each cutlet with a wooden or metal mallet. In a shallow bowl, combine breadcrumbs, Parmesan cheese, basil, parsley and pepper. Coat all sides of chicken with milk. Dredge chicken in breadcrumb mixture. Lightly coat toaster oven pan with vegetable oil. Place chicken on toaster oven pan and drizzle with remaining oil. Bake in a preheated 475° toaster oven for 6 to 7 minutes on each side.

Lay chicken on half of roll and cover with tomato sauce and mozzarella cheese. Cover with other roll half, wrap in foil and bake in a preheated 400° toaster oven for 10 minutes. Remove foil and serve immediately.

ITALIAN PLUM TOMATO SAUCE

Makes: 6 cups

This sauce is great with chicken, pasta and pizza. Keep the extra in small containers and store it in the freezer.

1 tbs. olive oil
2 clove garlic, minced or pressed
1 medium onion, finely chopped
2 cans (28 oz. each) Italian plum tomatoes, chopped or mashed, with juice
1 tbs. chopped fresh basil, or 1 tsp. dried
1 tsp. chopped fresh oregano, or 1/4 tsp. dried
1 bay leaf
1/4 tsp. pepper
1/4 tsp. salt

Heat olive oil in a medium saucepan over medium heat. Add garlic and onion and sauté over medium-low heat for 5 minutes, or until onion is soft. Add tomatoes. Stir in basil, oregano, bay leaf, pepper and salt. Partially cover saucepan. Reduce heat to low and simmer for at least 2 hours. Stir occasionally. Remove bay leaf and discard. Store covered in the refrigerator for a few days or in the freezer.

HOT PROSCIUTTO AND ARUGULA SANDWICH

Servings: 2

Look for arugula near the lettuce in your supermarket. Sometimes it's called roquette or arugula. It's a good idea to invest in an excellent-quality salad spinner for washing fresh leafy vegetables. Aside from the cutlery, it's perhaps the most utilized item in our test kitchen.

1 French roll, about 7 inches long
2 cups torn arugula leaves
2 artichoke hearts packed in water, drained and quartered
1 tbs. sliced black olives
4 slices prosciutto ham
2 tbs. *Pesto,* page 13, or commercially prepared pesto
$1/4$ tsp. dried oregano
$1/4$ tsp. dried sage
$1/8$ tsp. pepper

Slice roll in half lengthwise and lightly toast in the toaster oven. Distribute equal portions of arugula on bread slices. Top with artichoke hearts, olives and prosciutto. Spread pesto over prosciutto. Sprinkle with oregano, sage and pepper. Bake in a preheated 350° toaster oven for 10 minutes. Serve immediately.

DESSERTS

CHOCOLATE CHIP OATMEAL COOKIES

Makes: 12-15

This easy to prepare recipe makes incredibly rich and delicious chocolate chip cookies with a nice chewy texture. For additional fiber and nutrition, try making these cookies with whole-wheat flour.

1 cup packed light brown sugar
1½ tbs. canola oil
1 egg
½ cup applesauce
1 tsp. baking soda
1½ cups uncooked oatmeal

1½ cups all-purpose flour
2 tbs. cocoa powder
1 tsp. ground cinnamon
½ cup chopped walnuts
½ cup semisweet chocolate chips

With an electric mixer, beat sugar and oil. Add egg and applesauce; beat well until incorporated. In a medium bowl mix together baking soda, oats, flour, cocoa powder and cinnamon. Add flour mixture to sugar mixture; beat until dough forms. Add walnuts and chocolate chips; mix until blended. Drop teaspoons of cookie dough on toaster oven baking sheet about 2 inches apart. Bake in a preheated 350° oven for 10 to 12 minutes. Makes 12 to 15 cookies.

PINK CLOUDS

The heavenly aroma contributes to the name! Kids and adults go wild over this dessert.

1 frozen unbaked puff pastry sheet
1/2 cup fresh or frozen red raspberries
1/4 cup white chocolate chips
confectioners' sugar

Thaw sheet of pastry for 30 minutes. Use a rolling pin to flatten sheet into a 12-inch square. Divide sheet into four 6-inch square pieces. Place 2 tbs. raspberries and 1 tbs. white chocolate chips in the center of each piece of pastry. Bring corners of pastry together, pinch center and twist dough to seal. Press tops of puffs down, if necessary, so they do not touch the heating element in the toaster oven. Place pastry puffs on the toaster oven baking pan. Bake in a preheated 400° oven for 20 minutes. Remove from oven and sprinkle with confectioners' sugar. Cool for 5 to 10 minutes.

VARIATION

Fill each pastry puff with 1/4 cup 1-inch-thin apple slices, 1 tbs. maple syrup, 1 tsp. coarsely chopped walnuts and a sprinkle of cinnamon.

FRESH FRUIT CRISP

Here's a great dessert for kids and adults. This topping is also good over sliced apples and other fruits. You'll find a hand-held pastry blender to be a practical and time-saving kitchen tool when preparing this topping and other pastry recipes.

4 large fresh strawberries, stems removed, cut into ½-inch slices
½ cup fresh or frozen blueberries
1 large peach, cut into ½-inch slices
2 tsp. fresh lemon juice
¼ cup plus 2 tbs. flour
¼ cup brown sugar, firmly packed
¼ cup plus 2 tbs. oats

¼ tsp. cinnamon
⅛ tsp. nutmeg
¼ cup butter, cut into small pieces
1 tbs. sliced almonds
⅛ tsp. cinnamon
vanilla ice cream or whipped cream, optional

In a small bowl, combine fruit and lemon juice. Mix well. In a medium bowl, combine flour, brown sugar, oats, ¼ tsp. cinnamon and nutmeg. Mix well. Add butter and cut in until mixture looks like small peanuts. Place equal amounts of fruit mixture into 2 ovenproof ramekins and cover fruit with oatmeal topping. Sprinkle with almonds and cinnamon. Cover with foil and bake in a preheated 350° toaster oven for 35 minutes. Remove foil and bake for 5 more minutes. Top with vanilla ice cream or whipped cream.

ANISE SHORTBREAD

This elegant shortbread, with a hint of licorice flavor, goes well with coffee or tea and is quick and easy to bake. This recipe is based on a 4-slice toaster oven, but can easily be adjusted for large oven pans.

$\frac{1}{2}$ cup butter, softened
$\frac{1}{4}$ cup granulated sugar
$\frac{1}{4}$ cup confectioners' sugar
$\frac{1}{2}$ tsp. anise extract
1 cup flour

Cream butter and granulated sugar; gradually add confectioners' sugar and anise extract. Mix well. Add flour and blend thoroughly. Coat the toaster oven pan lightly with nonstick vegetable spray. Press dough firmly and evenly into pan. Poke the surface several times with a fork. Bake in a preheated 325° oven for 30 minutes, or until lightly golden brown. Remove from oven and let cool in pan for 5 to 10 minutes. Remove from pan and cut into 2-inch squares while still warm.

NUTTY SPONGE PUDDING

You'll get a lot of compliments when you serve this luscious, attractive dessert. And it's low in fat! Top with a whipped topping, or vanilla ice cream or frozen yogurt.

3 tbs. sugar
1/2 cup flour
1/2 tsp. baking powder
1/4 cup skim milk
2 tbs. butter, melted
1/4 cup light maple syrup
1/2 tsp. vanilla extract
3 tbs. chopped walnuts
1 apple peeled, cored and cut into 1/4-inch cubes

In a medium bowl, combine sugar, flour and baking powder. Stir in milk and butter. Mix well. Lightly coat two 5 1/2-inch round ovenproof baking dishes with nonstick vegetable spray. Pour equal amounts of batter into baking dishes. In a small bowl, combine maple syrup, vanilla, walnuts and apple cubes. Mix well. Distribute equally over batter. Bake in a pre-heated 350° toaster oven for 40 to 45 minutes. Serve hot with a favorite topping.

BEST EVER WALNUT BISCOTTI

For dessert, this biscotti always draws rave reviews. You can store biscotti in the freezer for up to 3 months before they get freezer burn. Just keep them protected tightly in plastic wrap, and then cover with foil. Defrost at room temperature for 30 minutes. Be sure to use a good quality of pure vanilla extract.

1¼ cups flour	½ cup sugar
1 tsp. baking powder	1 egg
pinch salt	1½ tsp. vanilla extract
2 tbs. butter, softened	½ cup coarsely chopped walnuts

Sift flour, baking powder and salt together. Set aside. With an electric mixer, cream butter and sugar. Add egg and mix well. Add vanilla and mix again. Add flour mixture and beat until completely blended. Mix in chopped walnuts. Form dough into a 9-x-5-inch loaf. Place loaf on a parchment paper-lined toaster oven pan and bake in a preheated 350° toaster oven for 35 minutes. Remove from oven and cool for 5 to 10 minutes on a wire rack. Cut into ¾-inch slices. Lay slices on the same parchment-lined oven pan and bake for 5 minutes. Turn slices over and bake for 5 additional minutes. Place cookies on a wire rack to cool and store in an airtight container.

APPLE GRAHAM NUT BAKE

This low fat dessert tastes as good as it looks. Serve it warm with a whipped topping or as is.

2 large apples
2 graham crackers
2 tsp. fresh lemon juice
2 tbs. light maple syrup
2 tbs. finely chopped walnuts
1/4 tsp. cinnamon
whipped topping, optional

Peel, core and slice apples into thin wedges. Crush graham crackers into crumbs. Place apple slices on the bottom of two oval ungreased individual ovenproof casseroles that measure about 4 1/2-x-7-x-1 1/2 inches. Cover apples with equal amounts of graham cracker crumbs. Drizzle lemon juice over cracker crumbs. Pour maple syrup over crumbs and sprinkle tops with walnuts and cinnamon. Bake in a preheated 425° toaster oven for 15 minutes. Serve warm with whipped topping.

BROWNIES

Here's a rich brownie with a recipe just the right size for your toaster oven. Some fat is cut from the usual brownie recipe, but you'll never miss what's missing.

1/4 cup low fat sweetened condensed milk
2 oz. unsweetened baking chocolate
1/3 cup semi sweet chocolate chips
2 egg whites
1 tbs. skim milk

1/2 tsp. vanilla extract
3 tbs. flour
3/4 tsp. baking powder
1/8 tsp. salt, optional
1/3 cup chopped walnuts or pecans

In a medium saucepan, combine sweetened condensed milk, unsweetened baking chocolate and chocolate chips. Heat over low heat or in a double boiler until chocolate is melted. Remove from stove. Add egg whites, skim milk and vanilla. Mix well. Add flour, baking powder and salt. Stir in walnuts. Spray toaster oven pan with nonstick vegetable spray and pour brownie batter evenly into pan. Bake in a preheated 350° toaster oven for 25 minutes. Remove from oven, let cool and cut into small square pieces.

CHOCOLATE CHIP MINI PIES

Servings: 4

Tired of the same old desserts? Treat yourself to a sense of adventure with a rich and interesting pie.

PIE CRUST
$^1/_2$ cup flour
$^1/_4$ tsp. salt
3 tbs. vegetable shortening
$1^1/_2$–2 tbs. water

Mix flour and salt together in a medium bowl. Use a pastry blender or fork to cut in shortening until the mixture resembles small peas. Drizzle with water and mix with a fork until dough is moistened and can be formed into a ball. Divide dough in quarters. Roll out dough to form four 6-inch circles, about $^1/_8$-inch thick. Place dough into four 4-inch tart pans or mini pie tins. Crimp edges of dough. Prick dough all over with the tines of a fork. Bake pie crusts in a preheated 425° toaster oven for 6 minutes, or until lightly brown.

CHOCOLATE FILLING

5 tbs. butter
¼ cup brown sugar, firmly packed
3 tbs. granulated sugar
¼ tsp. vanilla extract
1 egg
½ cup flour
¼ tsp. baking soda
3 oz. semisweet chocolate chips
¼ cup finely chopped walnuts

In a small saucepan over low heat, melt butter and add sugars; stir well. Remove from heat. Add vanilla, egg, flour and baking soda; stir well. Add chocolate chips and walnuts. Mix thoroughly. Pour mixture into pie crusts. Bake in a preheated 375° toaster oven oven for 20 to 25 minutes, or until a wooden pick inserted in the center of pie comes out clean.

APPLE CRISP

Apple crisp is always an absolutely delightful and memorable dessert. Serve it warm with ice cream, frozen yogurt or whipped topping.

2 large apples, peeled and cored
3/4 cup all-purpose flour
1/3 cup sugar
3/4 tsp. baking powder
1 egg white
2 tbs. butter, melted
1/8 tsp. cinnamon

Slice apples into 1/4-inch-thick wedges. In a medium bowl, combine flour, sugar, baking powder and egg white. Mix until texture of flour mixture looks like coarse crumbs or peanuts. Place equal amounts of apple wedges on the bottom of 2 round 5 1/2-x-2-inch ovenproof casseroles. Cover apples with equal amounts of crumb mixture. Drizzle with butter and sprinkle with cinnamon. Bake in a preheated 350° toaster oven for 35 minutes.

ANGEL LOAF

Serve this easy-to-make, fat-free loaf with a layer of fresh blueberries, sliced bananas, fresh sliced strawberries, or whipped topping and almond slivers.

6 egg whites
$3/4$ tsp. cream of tartar
$1/2$ tsp. vanilla extract
$1/2$ cup sugar
$1/2$ cup flour

In a large bowl, beat egg whites and cream of tartar until foamy. Mix in vanilla. Slowly add sugar and beat until stiff. Slowly fold in flour. Pour batter into a greased $8^1/2$-$4^1/2$-$2^1/2$-inch loaf pan. Cover loosely with a tent made from foil. Bake in a preheated 350° toaster oven for 30 minutes. Remove foil and bake for 15 more minutes. Let cool before serving.

TOASTER OVEN PANCAKE

Servings: 2

This delightful dessert can also be served as a richly special weekend breakfast or brunch dish. The batter can be made several hours in advance and refrigerated.

1½ tbs. sugar
½ cup flour
3 eggs, beaten
½ cup milk
1 tbs. butter
½ cup sliced fresh strawberries
maple syrup, warmed
confectioners' sugar

In a large bowl, mix together sugar and flour. Add beaten eggs to sugar and flour and mix well. Slowly add milk and beat well. Preheat toaster oven to 400°. Place butter in toaster oven pan. Melt butter and spread on all sides and bottom of pan. Pour pancake batter into pan and bake at 400° for 15 minutes. Reduce heat to 350° and bake for 25 more minutes. Remove pancake from pan and place on a small platter. Cover with sliced strawberries, drizzle with warmed maple syrup and sprinkle with confectioners' sugar. Serve warm.

INDEX

Serve Creative, Easy, Nutritious Meals with **nitty gritty**® Cookbooks

1 or 2, Cooking for
100 Dynamite Desserts
9 x 13 Pan Cookbook
Asian Cooking
Bagels, Best
Barbecue Cookbook
Beer and Good Food
Big Book Bread Machine
Big Book Kitchen Appliance
Big Book Snack, Appetizer
Blender Drinks
Bread Baking
New Bread Machine Book
Bread Machine III
Bread Machine V
Bread Machine VI
Bread Machine, Entrees
Burger Bible
Cappuccino/Espresso
Casseroles
Chicken, Unbeatable
Chile Peppers
Cooking in Clay

Coffee and Tea
Convection Oven
Cook-Ahead Cookbook
Crockery Pot, Extra-Special
Deep Fryer
Dehydrator Cookbook
Dessert Fondues
Edible Gifts
Edible Pockets
Fabulous Fiber Cookery
Fondue and Hot Dips
Fondue, New International
Freezer, 'Fridge, Pantry
Garlic Cookbook
Grains, Cooking with
Healthy Cooking on Run
Ice Cream Maker
Indoor Grill, Cooking on
Irish Pub Cooking
Italian, Quick and Easy
Juicer Book II
Kids, Cooking with Your
Kids, Healthy Snacks for

Loaf Pan, Recipes for
Low-Carb
No Salt No Sugar No Fat
Party Foods/Appetizers
Pasta Machine Cookbook
Pasta, Quick and Easy
Pinch of Time
Pizza, Best
Porcelain, Cooking in
Pressure Cooker
Rice Cooker
Salmon Cookbook
Sandwich Maker
Simple Substitutions
Slow Cooking
Slow Cooker, Vegetarian
Soups and Stews
Soy & Tofu Recipes
Tapas Fantásticas
Toaster Oven Cookbook
Waffles & Pizzelles
Wedding Catering book
Wraps and Roll-Ups

"Millions of books sold—for more than 35 years"   **For a free catalog, call:** **Bristol Publishing Enterprises**
(800) 346-4889
www.bristolpublishing.com